FRAMING THE POLICE ON TWITTER

This work assesses the various meanings attached to calls for police reform in the public discourse on social media, providing readers with a greater appreciation of the assumptions, empirical claims, and rhetorical nuances that underpin the current dialogue about police policy. Drawing upon an intersectional theoretical and mixed-methods approach, the authors look at what it means to "defund" or "abolish" the police, as well as the definition of community policing.

The death of George Floyd in 2020 resulted in national and international protests during which some members of the public began to demand "abolishing" or "defunding" the police, ideas previously put forth in academic arenas. However, these public protests were often presented in rhetorical ways that differed from the academic roots of the ideas. This book takes a deep look into what it means to "defund" or "abolish" the police, drawing upon academic origins of the concepts while at the same time examining how the public has used Twitter to define and discuss these ideas. The authors identify frameworks built around the concepts, discuss facts and perspectives that have contributed to these ideas, and explain how quantitative methods can be used to illustrate the most prominent frames.

This book incorporates both quantitative and qualitative means of research in an examination of Twitter and brings clarity to the conversation surrounding the "abolish the police", "defund the police", and "community policing" concepts. It is suitable for undergraduate to graduate-level college courses in criminology, sociology, policing, race in America, communication, social media, and research methods.

Benjamin Gross is Associate Professor of Sociology at St. Bonaventure University. He earned his PhD in Sociology from Michigan State University.

Samantha M. Gavin is Assistant Professor of Criminology at St. Bonaventure University. She earned her PhD in Criminology from Indiana University of Pennsylvania.

FRAMING THE POLICE ON TWITTER

Public Discourse on Abolishing Police, Defunding Police, and Community Policing

Benjamin Gross and Samantha M. Gavin

Routledge
Taylor & Francis Group

NEW YORK AND LONDON

Designed cover image: © Getty Images

First published 2024
by Routledge
605 Third Avenue, New York, NY 10158

and by Routledge
4 Park Square, Milton Park, Abingdon, Oxon, OX14 4RN

Routledge is an imprint of the Taylor & Francis Group, an informa business

© 2024 Benjamin Gross and Samantha M. Gavin

The right of Benjamin Gross and Samantha M. Gavin to be identified as authors of this work has been asserted in accordance with sections 77 and 78 of the Copyright, Designs and Patents Act 1988.

All rights reserved. No part of this book may be reprinted or reproduced or utilised in any form or by any electronic, mechanical, or other means, now known or hereafter invented, including photocopying and recording, or in any information storage or retrieval system, without permission in writing from the publishers.

Trademark notice: Product or corporate names may be trademarks or registered trademarks, and are used only for identification and explanation without intent to infringe.

ISBN: 978-1-032-12416-2 (hbk)
ISBN: 978-1-032-11780-5 (pbk)
ISBN: 978-1-003-22444-0 (ebk)

DOI: 10.4324/9781003224440

Typeset in Bembo
by Apex CoVantage, LLC

CONTENTS

PREFACE

Framing the Police on Twitter

On May 25, 2020, George Floyd died as a result of police abuse. This disturbingly violent incident was fully documented when it was recorded on a cell phone by an onlooker. The recording became rapidly distributed across the world via mass and social media, triggering anger among millions of people and leading to nationwide protests against police across the United States. Sadly, this was not the first time the public had seen visual footage of lethal police violence being directed toward an unarmed black man in the United States. This ongoing series of images documenting unjustifiable abuse, combined with the high repetition of these images being consumed by media audiences, led to widespread public outrage.

This collection of images shocked millions of Americans because many never have had any personal experiences of race-based violence at the hands of law enforcement and had never recognized this as a social problem. With people starting to demand change, social movements were fervently calling to either "abolish" or "defund" the police. These ideas were previously put forth in academic arenas but had really never been part of any nationwide dialogue. While it was clear that an angry and emotional public wanted sweeping reforms, it was unclear whether those engaging in protest really knew much about these policy initiatives.

Although criminologists and researchers had identified pros and cons of these concepts among themselves, protests had transformed these ideas primarily into chanted slogans that generally sounded like ambitious calls for change. But widely attended and heavily viewed public protests were introducing these terms to mass audiences exclusively in rhetorical ways, which often differed from their academic roots. This resulted in a disjointed public conversation about what police reform can, or should, look like. Thus, repeated calls to abolish and defund the police were being made by a wide variety of people in an unfocused and incoherent manner, proving to be confusing to media audiences and acting as a barrier to reform. The current level of ambiguity and politicization has stained these criminological approaches to police reform and has acted as a central motivation for why we have chosen to write this book.

Why This Book?

This book takes a deeper look into what it means to "defund" or "abolish" the police, as discussed by Twitter users, along with identifying how well the public understands the concept of "community policing". Drawing upon the academic origins of these theories, differences will be identified between the public's conceptualization of these ideas and the meanings endowed upon them by the original creators of these terms. The primary purpose is to illustrate not only how and why the public thinks about these ideas but also how the discussion of these ideas takes place within a public forum, such as Twitter.

This book is intended to provide readers with a greater appreciation of the assumptions, empirical claims, and rhetorical nuances which underpin public dialogue taking place regarding commonly referred to policies which target police reform.

Ultimately, there are three purposes for writing this book:

1. To examine societal perceptions regarding academic approaches to police reform

Two movements gained popularity during 2020, "Abolish The Police" and "Defund The Police". Each corresponding chapter examines the origins and intended meanings behind these policing ideas, which had been repurposed into slogans during the protest movements of 2020. This is followed by content analysis applied to 1,200 tweets made during June 2020, with special attention given toward the meanings constructed about these concepts by the US public. This sampling of tweets provided us with an ability to demonstrate the key meanings that have been constructed by Twitter users as these two social movements had progressed.

2. To compare and contrast between the original, academic-based origins of meaning with the public discourse pertaining to these concepts on Twitter

The book explores how Twitter users differ in the use of these terms from their original meanings, as intended by academic writers. Additionally, connections are made between social media content on Twitter and the influences which mass media news and politicians are able to make on these perceptions. By doing so, readers will be provided a more contextualized look into how the public may be influenced by external factors. This circumstance can lead people to hold inaccurate beliefs about law enforcement and these often-controversial police reform topics.

3. To engage in descriptive, exploratory research via content analyses to illustrate what people believe and feel about policing in the United States

Through a careful and systemic content analysis approach to analyzing 1,200 tweets made during June 2020, a detailed and vividly descriptive account of what people believe is documented in the upcoming chapters, often in the original wording of the content creators. While looking for factual claims being made by these authors, attention is given toward the expression of tone and emotion, focusing on what audiences are led to believe and feel within this discursive space.

Ultimately, our hope is to bring clarity and improve understanding to the public conversation surrounding the concepts of defunding the police, abolishing the police, and community policing. By helping to provide a better education of these policing policy approaches to audiences, the authors hope a more sophisticated public dialogue pertaining to these ideas will emerge in the future. Structured as an exploratory research study, this book strives to illuminate what people believe about these subjects, why they believe it, and what these content creators want other audience members to take away after viewing their messages.

In a democracy, what people believe and value are crucial to what laws they support and which policies are most likely to be implemented by our social institutions. In the United States, media content plays an important role regarding what people believe. People exchange meaning about objects and concepts with one another within a constellation of various forums, in both mediated and physical spaces, playing a central role in how one understands their social world. While debatable in terms of degree, it stands to reason that mediated communications should hold relatively strong influences on people due to the ubiquity of these messages in American life. On average, Americans spend about five and a half hours per day consuming visual medium content – watching television for about three hours – and using social media slightly more than two hours each day, according to recent research data (Stoll, 2022; Broadband Search, 2022). What people see and hear each day in these messages impacts what people define as problematic, what factors act as a cause to these social problems, and how much concern they have about an issue.

The next section discusses how sociological and communication theories can provide us with crucial tools for understanding how the social construction of meaning is impacted through the mediums we use each day. While the current media landscape offers a nearly infinite number of items which can serve as units of analysis, a scientific approach to the study of media content requires a theoretically principled and systematic approach. For our purposes, media frames are directly useful for theorizing how and why various discourses are advanced. Likewise, it provides a logical and well-tested approach for deconstructing media texts found in virtually any forum, allowing us to uncover how Twitter users interpret problematic policing and reform. The next section intends to clarify various media studies concepts and terminologies that are relevant to what we will recurrently be referring to throughout this book.

Mediated Experiences and Public Discourse

As we will discuss further in the next chapter, media content acts as a "window to the world" (Coombs, 1965), giving people a glimpse about social realities which exist beyond our own personal experiences. This window is especially relevant as it pertains to interactions with police, an experience with which most Americans have little-to-no direct experience (Surette, 2015). Mediated content provides people with vicarious experiences, where they can reflect on how they would think and feel had they been placed in a given situation. For Americans, high levels of exposure to movies, television shows, books, radio, magazines, and news broadcasts (among others) can expand the horizons of audiences – and are likely to influence beliefs and behavior in areas where viewers have no prior frames of reference (Klapper, 1960).

While the expansion of mass medium channels became a common feature of daily life during the 20th century, the 21st century has seen the massive growth of internet usage among the public, being a common resource for everyday Americans to frequently interact with one another. In virtually all modern Western democracies, the internet serves as a public sphere. Due to the structure of the internet, where there are few barriers to entry for users and low levels of censorship, it can theoretically act as an ideal space for the open exchange of ideas. The internet is viewed by social theorists as being crucial to the health of democracies, necessary to help citizens understand public issues and develop informed collective responses to them. Social theorists often view the internet in an idealized fashion, which can lead to improvements in informational quality, increased levels of activism, and fostering a sense of community (Rheingold, 2000; Benkler, 2006; Castells, 2010; Rainie & Wellman, 2012).

Our primary research interest is to observe the discourse of policing within an online "public sphere", defined as any public space where individuals can freely discuss societal problems collectively (Habermas, 1989, p. 136). While the internet is far too vast to fully examine and interpret, the highly popular social media platform "Twitter" is ideally suited for discursive research. Twitter is an online space where users are afforded the ability to express themselves freely in addressing public issues in both affective and rational terms. It is an interactive space where people feel that their views matter to others, which Zizi Papacharissi (2015) refers to as an "Affective Public" (p. 4). Social media contributors on Twitter hold the ability to make emotive declarations online through their own words, photos, and videos. In turn, users are able to react to this content and discuss the same issue while simultaneously feeling as though they have become a part of the issue (Papacharissi, 2015).

As Twitter users construct postings which relay facts and opinions around an issue, they are also forming assumptions and definitions around those claims, which are often referred to in media studies as frames. Media scholars have used frame analysis widely over the last 40 years across a wide array of media texts as a way of explaining how the public learns and interprets social issues (Tversky & Kahneman, 1981; Entman, 1993; Kuypers, 2006). George Lakoff (2004) describes frames as analogous to cognitive maps, impacting how viewers believe they should recognize, understand, and process information. Previous research on media frames has identified how they impact public understanding of a wide array of social and political issues, such as labor disputes (Martin, 2003), nuclear energy policy (Gamson & Modigliani, 1989), war in the Middle East (Kuypers, 2006; Butler, 2009), affirmative action (Gamson & Modigliani, 1989), and beliefs regarding race and poverty (Iyengar, 1991; Entman & Rojecki, 2000; Gilens, 2000; Kendall, 2011).

What Are Media Frames?

The concept of a frame is based on the idea of a picture: a frame structures and organizes the pieces of a photo together into a meaningful coherence, helping a person understand what he or she is experiencing. Frames help us see and understand the picture; they channel our attention, and impact our perceptions but also lead us to ignore information which falls to the outside of it. Frames, in short, structure our ideas and reasoning (Gitlin, 1980; Gamson & Modigliani, 1989; Lakoff, 2007; Luntz, 2007). They are found within narrative accounts of issues and events, acting as the central organizing idea of a story (Lakoff, 2004; Kuypers, 2006; Luntz, 2007).

In his classic book *Frame Analysis*, Erving Goffman (1974) discussed how the minds of human beings rely on frameworks to understand and interpret the social world. Goffman thought of a frame mainly in cognitive terms, viewing it as a set of concepts and theoretical perspectives which help people organize experiences. However, frames can also be found in media messages, where an author purposely packages and presents information in ways which encourage certain interpretations and discourage others to influence audiences into a desired position. Media frames operate in four key ways: they (1) define problems, (2) diagnose causes, (3) make moral judgments, and (4) suggest remedies to the problem at hand. They are found within narrative media accounts of issues or events, typically as the central organizing idea of a story, deeply impacting how people interpret sociopolitical issues (Kuypers, 2006).

Not only are frames vitally important for understanding how Americans understand issues, but also they are crucial for the success of political debates. Those who are able to create and maintain frames built around their own assumptions and viewpoints will be able to control political discourse and the ways in which the general public thinks about social issues (Lakoff, 2004; Luntz, 2007). While the recipients of mediated messages hold the ability to reject or transform the frames imposed on them in the marketplace of ideas through an engagement in critical reasoning (Thompson, 1995), they often do not. Recipients often lack the motivation or time to engage in challenging claims and assumptions presented to them, tending to adapt the frames uncritically, making them a powerful feature in public persuasion. Likewise, the readers of media texts tend to accept only the facts which fit within the framework of a discussion. Social scientists have repeatedly found that framing can effectively sway how people make decisions and alter beliefs, changing intended courses of action across a myriad of social contexts (Tversky & Kahneman, 1981; Iyengar, 1991; Gilens, 2000; Luntz, 2007; Butler, 2009; Kendall, 2011).

Throughout this book, we will illustrate what claims Twitter users are highlighting and overlooking in their postings when they discuss policing. Factual claims that are being voiced will be covered and occasionally challenged in terms of accuracy. Likewise, expressions which are designed to evoke emotionally charged interpretations among audience members will be deconstructed to decipher what desired interpretations audiences are being persuaded to adopt. Overall, we believe that we have uncovered a variety of important beliefs and opinions held by the public about what people think are the causes and remedies to controversial police practices.

Of course, the media landscape in the United States is staggeringly enormous. The overall public dialogue regarding policing in the United States spans across all medium channels and platforms, being impossible to fully comprehend in its entirety. As a result, we have limited our research attention to Twitter, a highly popular social media platform with millions of users, where social topics can be discussed and learned about at any time of day or night. With this in mind, the next section turns the reader's attention to our research plan, explaining how we sampled Twitter content, which categories were coded into variables, and how reliable those measures were.

Methodology

The data used in this study come from the collection of 1,200 tweets which were posted online between June 1 and June 10, 2020, and Twitter's advanced search feature was used to locate this content. The first sample contained the use of the hashtag #AbolishThePolice, the second sample referring to #DefundThePolice, and the third using #CommunityPolicing. Given that the tweets mentioning "defund" and "abolish" were being produced at a higher volume than community policing, a decision was made to sample in disproportionate group sizes. In the overall sample, 500 tweets referring to "abolish", 500 tweets referring to "defund", and 200 tweets using the hashtag "community policing" were selected. The tweets sampled for this project were based on what the researcher was exposed to first and then read continuously through a scroll of successive postings, in an effort to mimic the likely surfing pattern of a typical user's experience.

We purposely selected this time period as it was a peak for public attention and concern about the need for police reform, which created a high frequency of tweets becoming available for analysis. Twitter users were clearly emotional about the events taking place, often taking place in real time, which were unfolding on their screens. This period served as a unique opportunity to uncover, in more detail than would otherwise be captured, how people felt about law enforcement and how people understood these police reform concepts in their own words.

Each tweet was coded using a combination of manifest and latent content analysis technique as described by Klaus Krippendorff (2012). Categories pertaining to the expression of anger by the writer, perceptions about the approval/disapproval of policing, beliefs about racism among the

TABLE 0.1 Variables Used in Manifest Coding System

Variable Name	Description	Coding Values
Anger	Does writer exhibit anger toward police?	0=No, 1=Yes
Cop Oppose	How does writer evaluate the police?	−1=Negatively
		0=Neutrally
		+1=Positively
Racist	Are police accused of being racist?	0=No, 1=Yes
Reform	Does author believe police	−1=No
	can be reformed?	0=Not Answered
		+1=Yes
Violent	Are police accused or shown	0=No, 1=Yes
	being violent?	

police, the likelihood of reform, and accusations of police violence were measured quantitatively. Specifics regarding how these variables were coded can be seen in Table 0.1.

Additionally, three subsamples (one containing 25 tweets from *#AbolishThePolice* hashtag, another 25 from *#DefundThePolice*, as well as 25 coming from *#CommunityPolicing*) were randomly selected to measure inter-coder reliability. To measure reliability, we used two approaches. The first was an overall general accuracy rate based on the percentage of times the same code was recorded by both users and the other being a more sophisticated probability-based measure called Cohen's kappa.

Reliability results from the *#AbolishThePolice* subsample indicated that the general accuracy rate equaled 0.80, with a Cohen's kappa score of 0.53. Also, the *#DefundThePolice* subsample had a general accuracy rate of 0.903, with a Cohen's kappa score equal to 0.715. Lastly, the *#Community-Policing* subsample scored a general accuracy rate of 0.76, with a Cohen's kappa score equal to 0.476. Overall, we were satisfied with these results, as Cohen's kappa values ranging between 0.40 and 0.75 are interpreted as having "fair to good" inter-rater agreement levels, which are likely to be occurring beyond random chance (Fleiss et al., 2003).

Overview of the Book

Our outlay deems it imperative to discuss these concepts separately from one another and also allow for comparisons to be made, as we examine differences between concepts, as well as variations between competing frameworks that are embedded in the same discourse. Within each chapter, a detailed examination of how the public defined and discussed these concepts within the identified Twitter hashtag is covered. The following is a quick chapter-by-chapter summary of this book.

Chapter 1: The Origins of Policing and Media Depictions of Law Enforcement

The purpose of this chapter is to introduce the reader to the history of policing in the United States, as well as how law enforcement has historically been depicted in American media. Reviewing the social and historical context of how people in the United States have constructed expectations around policing, both through public policies and through their consumption of mediated content, impacts how beliefs and attitudes about law enforcement have been formed by people. A familiarity with this background is imperative for understanding what people feel about law enforcement during the summer of 2020, which impacts the content Twitter users were sharing.

Chapter 2: Abolish the Police on Twitter

The chapter begins with a review pertaining to the academic and activist origins of "abolish the police" and how experts view the concept as currently being relevant and applicable to policing in the United States. Next, we use primarily qualitative analysis of data to outline six frameworks that were found to coexist within the discourse, illustrating how "abolish the police" is packaged in media content by Twitter users. The most prevalent Twitter frames emerging from this 500-tweets sample were collected, analyzed, and described in detail, where we also make comparisons and contrasts to the other frames which were also embedded within this discourse.

Chapter 3: Defund the Police on Twitter

Analogous to the previous chapter, a review of what various contributors have meant by the phrase "defund the police" is explored. Likewise, we use qualitative analysis of 500 tweets using the hashtag *#DefundThePolice* to explain with rich detail how various content creators on Twitter depicted what it means to defund the police in their own words. Ultimately, four frameworks were found within this discourse. We describe each in detail, illustrating how various writers make differing claims and assumptions within these messages in an attempt to influence readers about the current state of policing in the United States.

Chapter 4: Public Discourse and the Nature of Community Policing

In contrast to the progressive "abolish" and "defund" concepts in the previous two chapters, calls for a return to an earlier era of "community policing" are provided in Chapter 4, as community policing has once again returned to the forefront of policy discussions. In this chapter, the history of policing in the United States is reviewed, placing this concept within the proper context of a practice that waxed and waned in a long process of public preferences. This section provides the reader with an evolution of community policing, detailing its origins, why it once emerged as a preferred form of policing, and why the nation largely moved away from its usage in the 1990s. This review is followed by frame analysis of the public's perceptions of what community policing means, as it is described on Twitter, within a sampling to 200 tweets. The analysis indicates that the American public tends to have a false idea of just what community policing actually entails and often conflates it with various other policing approaches.

Chapter 5: Summary and Conclusions

The final chapter reviews and highlights the main findings of this book. We review and summarize what people believe about community policing, defunding the police, and abolishing the police. This chapter moreover discusses the nature and tone of the discourse, with implications for how these factors impact public beliefs. Additionally, we expound on how mass media and politics may be acting as barriers to public understanding of these terms and, ultimately, to the likelihood of police reform.

References

Benkler, Y. (2006). *The wealth of networks: How social production transforms markets and freedom.* Yale University Press.

Broadband Search. (2022). *Average daily time spent on social media.* www.broadbandsearch.net/blog/average-daily-time-on-social-media#post-navigation-1

Butler, J. (2009). *Frames of war: When is life grievable?* Verso Publishing.

Castells, M. (2010). *The rise of the network society* (2nd ed.). Wiley-Blackwell.

Coombs, C. I. (1965). *Window on the world. The story of television production.* The World Publishing Company.

Entman, R. M. (1993). Framing: Toward clarification of a fractured paradigm. *Journal of Communication, 43*(4), 51–58.

Entman, R. M., & Rojecki, A. (2000). *The black image in the white mind: Media and race in America.* University of Chicago Press.

Fleiss, J. L., Levin, B., & Cho Paik, M. (2003). *Statistical rates for rates and propositions* (3rd ed.). Wiley-Interscience Publishing.

Gamson, W. A., & Modigliani, A. (1989). Media discourse and public opinion on nuclear power: A constructionist approach. *American Journal of Sociology, 95*(1), 1–37.

Gilens, M. (2000). *Why Americans hate welfare: Race, media, and the politics of antipoverty policy.* University of Chicago Press.

Gitlin, T. (1980). *The whole world is watching: Mass media in the making and unmaking of the new left.* University of California Press.

Goffman, E. (1974). *Frame analysis: An essay on the organization of experience.* Northeastern University Press.

Habermas, J. (1989). *The structural transformation of the public sphere: An inquiry into a category of Bourgeois society.* Polity Press.

Iyengar, S. (1991). *Is anyone responsible?* University of Chicago Press.

Kendall, D. (2011). *Framing class: Media representations of wealth and poverty in America* (2nd ed.). Rowman & Littlefield Publishing.

Klapper, J. (1960). *The effects of mass communication.* Free Press.

Krippendorff, K. (2012). *Content analysis: An introduction to its methodology* (3rd ed.). Sage Publications.

Kuypers, J. A. (2006). *Bush's war: Media bias and justifications for war in a terrorist age.* Rowman & Littlefield Publishers.

Lakoff, G. (2004). *Don't think of an elephant: Know your values and frame the debate.* Chelsea Green Publishers.

Luntz, F. (2007). *Words that work: It's not what you say, it's what people hear.* Hyperion Books.

Martin, C. R. (2003). *Framed! Labor and the corporate media.* Cornell University Press.

Papacharissi, Z. (2015). *Affective publics: Sentiment, technology and politics.* Oxford University Press.

Rainie, L., & Wellman B. (2012). *Networked: The new social operating system.* MIT Press.

Rheingold, H. (2000). *The virtual community: Homesteading on the virtual frontier.* MIT Press.

Stoll, J. (2022). Average daily time spent watching TV in America. *Statistica.* www.statista.com/statistics/186833/average-television-use-per-person-in-the-us-since-2002/

Surette, R. (2015). *Media, crime, and criminal justice: Images, realities, and policies.* Thomas Wadsworth Publishing.

Thompson, J. B. (1995). *The media and modernity: A social theory of the media.* Stanford University Press.

Tversky, A., & Kahneman, D. (1981). The framing of decisions and the psychology of choice. *Science, 211*(4481), 453–458.

1

MEDIA DEPICTIONS OF LAW ENFORCEMENT

Introduction

Today, there are over 650,000 full-time law enforcement officers in the United States, according to the U.S. Bureau of Labor Statistics (2021). In a democratic nation, what people believe about their police force impacts virtually all aspects of law enforcement, including what day-to-day operations the public considers to be acceptable practices. When the public is dissatisfied with policing, they hold the ability to demand reforms and may pursue pressure toward the institution via reducing the amount of labor and money invested into these forces. In this social context, it is highly important for law enforcement officers and agencies to maintain a positive image to maintain economic stability and credibility with the public. In the United States, where the large consumption of mediated images is a ubiquitous facet of daily life, mediated content is crucial in the formation and maintenance of public beliefs and opinions. With this fact in mind, we turn our attention toward how law enforcement has historically been depicted in various media genres, and how these various messages have produced complex, inconsistent, and unclear beliefs about the police in the minds of the public.

Media Effects and Policing

A century ago, Walter Lippmann in his classic book *Public Opinion* described media content as crucial for modern people to understand their social world. Through streams of mediated images, which form "pictures in our heads" of various people and events that are taking place around us, people feel they can construct meaning of things which exist beyond their own personal experiences. For the majority of Americans, a large percentage of the mediated content comes in the form of television, as the presence of television is ubiquitous in daily American life. Television has been described as "society's storyteller" (Gerbner, 1993, p. 3), where "television tells most of the stories, to most of the people, most of the time". These stories are central to how people socially construct reality (Berger & Luckmann, 1966), as these messages tell us facts and figures, and explain how things work – playing a crucial role in how we determine truth (Gerbner, 1993).

Ultimately, however, media depictions of reality are inherently oversimplified, subjective, and flawed, where audiences will unavoidably form misperceptions about their social world. Lippmann

DOI: 10.4324/9781003224440-1

(2020) described the mental images we construct as a "pseudo-environment", an abstraction of reality, which is a fiction that we perceive to be real. Nevertheless, as social theorist W.I. Thomas once stated, "If men define situations as real, they are real in their consequences" (Stryker, 1980, p. 6). In other words, even if the world we perceive is not objective reality, it will still be relevant to the actions and behaviors of audiences, who act on what they believe.

Iconic theorists such as these inspired the study of media effects research, who were motivated by the desire to understand how mediated messages can shape public opinion and be relevant to explaining behavior. Researchers have found that mediated content pertaining to police officers are salient to public attitude formation, impacting perceptions of police legitimacy, accountability, and levels of citizen compliance toward law enforcement (Intravia et al., 2017; Tyler, 2004).

With regard to the formation of beliefs and opinions the public holds toward crime and law enforcement officers, there is good reason to believe media content has a considerable effect on audiences, with important ramifications for policing and public policy. For one, most Americans have not had any direct personal experiences with the police. It has been estimated that only about 20 percent of Americans have had an interaction with a police officer, and nearly half of those incidents were for traffic violation stops (Surette, 2015; Eith & Durose, 2011; Langton & Durose, 2013; Choi et al., 2020). Since a majority of the public has a very limited frame of reference for evaluating policing in the United States, their beliefs and attitudes are considered to be informed primarily by the media content they consume. This viewpoint is consistent with the principles of media theorist Joseph Klapper (1960), who stated that media effects were likely to be strongest in situations where people have had no other previous personal experiences. When audiences lack other points of reference, the effects of media content are more likely to be strong, with a greater likelihood of influencing opinions and behaviors of audiences.

Although a large percentage of the American public does not have direct relationships or experiences with the police, they do spend several hours a day using mass and social media. As measured in terms of time use per day, watching television has long been the most common leisure activity for Americans for many years, spending on average 2.8 hours per day watching television (U.S. Bureau of Labor Statistics, 2015). In return, individuals receive the majority of their knowledge about crime and the criminal justice system from the media, and their attitudes and beliefs on these topics are shaped by media consumption (Intravia et al., 2017). It is believed that the media plays a significant role in structuring views about the police, as a substantial proportion of the US public is exposed to large amounts of mass media content each day. Stories about crime received enormous amount of public attention, having been estimated to comprise as much as one-third of contemporary media content (McCall, 2007).

Media effects on public perceptions of the police have received a fair amount of attention because mass media is recognized as one of the resources for information about crime (Choi et al., 2020; Graziano, 2018; Dowler, 2002; Dowler & Zawilski, 2007). Scholars have long noted that media content plays a role in shaping American's attitudes about crime and justice (Donovan & Klahm, 2015), as the public often holds distorted beliefs about crime based on media consumption (Chiricos et al., 2000; Dowler, 2002; Dowler & Zawilski, 2007; Colbran, 2014). For example, it has been found that citizens mainly rely on media information as a resource for judgments about the police and often form their perceptions of the police independent of real-world experiences (Choi et al., 2020). Indeed, most Americans today obtain news and other information regarding crime through various mediums, including television, newspaper, and social media platforms (Shearer & Matsa, 2018).

As a result, social scientists have spent several decades conducting research about how crime and law enforcement are represented in mass media programs and how this content influences the beliefs and attitudes of viewers. This large body of research has produced a highly complex and often contradictory set of findings regarding depictions of the police, as well as if, and how, this content impacts how the public feels about them. In the upcoming section, we will summarize the existing literature on this topic and then link it to the more recent interest in studying the relationship between police and social media use.

Early Research and Uniform Effects: Cultivation Theory

During the 1970s, Cultivation Theory (Gerbner & Gross, 1976) emerged as the first major media effects conceptualization which provided insight into how the viewing of crime on television impacted public beliefs about crime, policing, and social order. What Gerbner and his colleagues (1980, 1986) proposed was that television viewing created a "mainstreaming" effect onto audience members – or that viewer beliefs about crime rates would converge across all audience demographics. In other words, the more that a person watched television, the more their perceptions will match what is most frequently depicted in the media and sharing these beliefs about crime with all other television viewers, regardless of differences in the age, race, social class, or personal experiences between users. On a macro-level scale, as millions of Americans continued to watch more and more television each day, year after year, the public is expected to develop shared beliefs about crime in the United States. The audience develops a worldview that matches certain media images and messages rather than social reality (Custers & Van den Bulck, 2013).

Moreover, Cultivation Theory proposed that television content sensationalized crime and exaggerated the amount of crime that was actually taking place, leading viewers to hold distorted beliefs and the prevalence of crime in society. Gerbner referred to this as "Mean World Syndrome" (Gerbner & Gross, 1976; Gerbner et al., 1978, 1980, 1986; Eschholz et al., 2003; Roche et al., 2016), claiming that those who watched several hours of television each day would become fearful about crime, believing that danger was everywhere, and that the likelihood of becoming a victim of crime was excessively high. Gerbner hypothesized that high levels of daily television viewing would influence the public toward conservative values, who perceived that social order in the United States was in peril and that it needed to be reestablished by expanding law enforcement to both prevent crimes and effectively prosecute criminals (Gerbner & Gross, 1976).

While Cultivation Theory does not specifically predict how people would feel about the police, it presumed that watching television would produce more public support for law enforcement, in general, due to their exaggerated fears about crime. It purported that the heightened levels of crime media content instilled fear into audiences, leading the public to rely more on the police and to increase both the confidence in the police (Choi et al., 2020) and the level of importance held by the public toward law enforcement (Skogan, 2009). Research being produced under the Cultivation theoretical paradigm expected to find that viewers would strongly and consistently support police practices and hold favorable opinions toward police officers. Viewers would want to see the police attain more empowerment (in terms of budget spending and expanded legal rights) to effectively reduce crime and bring about social order.

However, the empirical research produced under the central tenets of Cultivation Theory produced highly mixed results in a variety of ways. First, research found that the correlations between television viewing and perceptions of law enforcement were often small, insignificant, or even opposite of what was predicted (Gauthier & Graziano, 2018). On the one hand, those who watched more of television consistently had distorted views about crime rates being higher than they actually were (Choi et al., 2020), held increased fears about crime (Chiricos et al., 1997; Weitzer & Kubrin, 2004; Intravia et al., 2017; Choi et al., 2020), and also supported more punitive crime policies (Gilliam & Iyengar, 2000; Callanan & Rosenberger, 2011; Gauthier & Graziano, 2018). In contrast, viewers did not consistently exhibit more positive or negative confidence in the police (Gauthier & Graziano, 2018), often holding ambivalent feelings, as well as feelings of disappointment in the police in terms of efficacy at fighting crime (Hinds & Murphy, 2007; Van Craen, 2013). For example, conservatives were less likely to believe the police are successfully combating crime, yet held higher expectations for police conduct than did other viewers of police content (Donovan & Klahm, 2015).

Findings like these raised questions about whether mainstreaming was occurring among audiences. While Cultivation Theory proposed that television viewing would be the prime influence in the formation of beliefs and attitudes viewers had about law enforcement, it turned out that there were other factors that were more important, such as demographic factors, personal experiences, and neighborhood contexts (Tuch & Weitzer, 1997; Intravia et al., 2017; Callanan & Rosenberger, 2011; Weitzer & Tuch 2004; Fridkin et al., 2017; Choi et al., 2020). For example, researchers found that racial minorities held consistently more negative opinions about the police regardless of their viewing habits, with the same also being true for younger viewers (Weitzer & Tuch, 1999; Dowler, 2002; Dowler & Zawilski, 2007; Weitzer & Tuch, 2004; Callanan & Rosenberger, 2011). Likewise, those who had first-hand experiences with police officers also expressed more negative feelings about the police, as did those who were living in high-crime neighborhoods, who often believed that the police were ineffective at enforcing the law (Dowler, 2002; Intravia et al., 2017; Choi et al., 2020). Moreover, those who perceived crime as being excessively high in their area were prone to concluding that the police were incompetent, or otherwise ineffective at fighting crime, indicating reduced support for law enforcement (Dowler, 2002; Jackson & Sunshine, 2007; Jackson et al., 2009; Wu, 2014; Intravia et al., 2017). Although research was indicating that while media content was likely to play some role in how people felt about crime and policing, the size of the effect had come into question, and it had also become clear that these media effects were not uniform across the audience. The picture that emerged is that there are important audience traits that, when combined with media consumption, are likely to produce differing cultivation patterns (Intravia et al., 2017).

Also, it had become evident that the kind of content the viewer was consuming made a difference. While Gerbner believed that simply being exposed to television content over time would lead to shared perceptions about crime and law enforcement, the ways in which the police were represented in fictional content such as movies and television shows varied from news broadcasts. With this in mind, media effects researchers began to differentiate between various genres, noting that fiction and nonfictional content tended to produce varying representations about police and their practices.

Conditional Media Effects: Accounting for Variability in Audiences and Sources

In response to the lack of universal effects proposed by Cultivation Theory, research focus began to place a greater attention to account for variance among audience member characteristics, as well as on the creators of message content. The idea that media messages would have a uniform effect on all audience members had proven to be an oversimplification and overlooked the fact that media content is not the only factor in a person's understanding of the social world. Contemporary media research efforts have disaggregated media audiences, learning to make comparisons both between and within audiences. Media effects vary, being conditionally based on differing personal backgrounds, social identities, previous levels of knowledge or expertise, as well as having varied levels of personal experience with police and crime. By accounting for these important differences, research can provide a more compelling, albeit much more complex, illustration into how exposure to content may impact attitudes and perceptions (Chiricos et al., 1997; Roche et al., 2016; Weitzer & Tuch, 2004; Intravia et al., 2017).

With regard to sources and genres, research has noted that police are often portrayed differently based on the type of media in question. To better understand mediated meaning construction of crime and police, attention toward various message sources, as well as upon the creators of content, is believed to provide insight into public understanding of law enforcement (Intravia et al., 2017). What are audiences learning about how policing is practiced? Do audiences believe that the police were effective at catching criminals? What do viewers believe about the motives and morality of police officers, and why? Is police violence necessary or not? As it turns out, the kinds of mass media content that a person is consuming, as well as who is producing that content, provide differing answers to these questions. As a result, the public is continually exposed to mixed messages about policing – which often leads to a public whose opinions about the police are inconsistent, ambivalent, and often contradictory.

One form of source differentiation is to focus on "Claimsmakers", which sociologist Joel Best (2016) defines as the people who are constructing the media messages that are consumed by mass audiences. Claimsmakers create messages to make claims about what they perceive to be social reality – producing messages which package objective facts with subjective judgments to persuade public opinion and potentially motivate people into acting. With regard to mass media and policing, the most common claimsmakers tend to be journalists, law enforcement experts (such as politicians, officers, and police departments), as well as fictional writers, celebrities, social activists, and members of the general public affected by crime.

Messengers with access to mass media channels communicate to the public by employing rhetorical strategies, such as in the development of frames to define a public problem while also utilizing their own perspectives in identifying its main cause. These messages often include arguments which rely on normative judgments to define how a situation should be addressed, as well as identifying who is responsible to remedy the issue. The mass media environment in which we live is filled with a nearly countless number of claims about crime and policing, where public dialogue includes many perspectives, assumptions, and factual claims. Nevertheless, some types of claimsmakers have more access to mass mediums, which make these people more likely to shape public opinion and policy.

Police practices are often described and explained in a variant manner depending on who is constructing the mass-mediated content – where the three premier groups of claimsmakers are journalists, law enforcement officers, and fiction writers. These messages are received in a highly variant manner, depending on whether the messages are produced in either a fictional or a nonfictional context, such as news programs. Crime and police are depicted significantly differently in television news broadcasts and fiction-based entertainment programs within these genres, in part, because different claimsmakers are more prevalent within these specific areas. These varying accounts over crime, policing, and social problems pertaining to each can lead mass media audiences toward divergent beliefs about law enforcement.

News Media Coverage: Police and Crime

Scholars have long recognized that news matters in how we perceive events in our social world (Iyengar & Kinder, 2010; McCombs et al., 2011), including our understanding of police (Graziano, 2018). Those who study contemporary mass media television news effects place their attention on two general areas – factors which influence the production of news programs and organizational conventions in content presentations to audiences. Research on the practice of news production emphasizes how journalists must rely on official sources for a consistent supply of enough informational content to construct a news broadcast each day (Dunaway & Graber, 2022; McCombs et al., 2011). By doing so, institutional official holders and other high-status newsmakers are believed to hold an advantaged position in the construction of news content, being more available than other potential claimsmakers to have their perspectives voiced in these broadcasted programs. Additionally, the current 24-hour news cycle creates endless pressures on journalists to produce news stories extremely quickly. It has been said by critics that these never-ending time pressures continually place journalists and news organizations in situations where they are tempted to engage in cutting corners on fact-checking and investigative reporting, threatening news quality for audiences and undermining public trust (Downie & Kaiser, 2003; Rosenberg, 2009; Schudson, 2011).

Compounding the news content production decisions are the limits of television news being a visual medium, where attention-grabbing dramatic footage often takes precedence over verbal forms of information in the selection of news content (Iyengar & Kinder, 2010; Dunaway & Graber, 2022). Likewise, the limited amount of time available to cover a range of stories requires coverage to present oversimplified accounts that lack any contextual grounding or in-depth examinations of videos and stories. Researchers have claimed that encourages an "if it bleeds, it leads" approach to content production, where visual footage of violence, extreme behaviors, and police chases are disproportionately more likely to be selected as being newsworthy. Just as problematic is that this footage is difficult to place in context, which often distorts these events in the minds of viewers – creating misunderstanding, visceral emotion-based reactions, and outrage (Taibbi, 2020).

The other body of research focuses on organizational conventions – emphasizing that the social and economic context of mass media news production is based primarily on for-profit incentives by news media corporations. To attain maximized profits, these companies must intensely compete for viewership with a large quantity of other viewing options available to audience members. These economic pressures are largely believed to have a detrimental effect on news construction and for public beliefs and opinions. Programmers gear their decisions about newsworthiness toward the sensational and the unusual and to address topics that are controversial using confrontational language and formats. This format is especially true for cable news networks and political talk shows – many of which rank as the most viewed broadcasts in the United States. Recent research has outlined how news broadcasts often attempt to maximize audiences, and therefore profits, by selecting and constructing content which will appeal to politically segmented like-minded audiences. As a result, these broadcasts are often accused of purposely politicizing events, to adapt in-group political values and preexisting beliefs to placate or reinforce the audience's existing beliefs as a way to generate consistent viewership. Tactics often include using inflammatory language to belittle the perspectives and claims of political opponents. Many of these broadcasts act more as a form of infotainment that distorts public beliefs and reinforce attitudinal extremity among viewers (Berry & Sobieraj, 2016; Altheide, 2015; Taibbi, 2020). Television news programs are often presented using a form of "Media Logic" (Altheide, 2015), which offers discourse of issues that mimic a win/loss sports competition format. Within this delivery context, audiences view debates which take the form of aggressive argumentation that encourages using oversimplified sound bites and discourages listening or compromise (Altheide 2015; Berry & Sobieraj, 2016; Taibbi, 2020).

Taken in combination, these limitations on news broadcast organizations by current journalistic practices and economic pressures do not bode well for the quality of news programming. Nevertheless, there is an extremely high amount of news content available to the public today across a wide variety of mass and social mediums – including an array of news about crime and policing which is largely produced within these news production contexts. While these forces harm public understanding about policing and crime, the size of news audiences for this content remains large, even though trust in news institutions has sharply declined in recent years. For example, a recent study by Gallup found that the American news media organizations are the second least trusted US institutions of the 16 that the public were asked about. Only 11 percent of Americans expressed confidence in the news media, finishing only ahead of congress, whose approval rating was 7 percent (Jones, 2022).

In nonfiction depictions of crime and policing, network television news reports often do not portray the police in a positive light, with stories which commonly draw public attention toward examples of misconduct and corruption (Donovan & Klahm, 2015; Gauthier & Graziano, 2018; Weitzer & Tuch, 2004; Intravia et al., 2017). While there is some research which indicates that television news viewers, especially those who prefer local news programs, show more trust and support toward the police (Eschholz et al., 2003; Callanan & Rosenberger, 2011; Gauthier & Graziano, 2018), research identifies more instances where viewing creates disapproval for law enforcement, particularly when troubling aspects about police behavior exist within these stories. Likewise, individuals who frequently consumed television network news were found by some to be more likely to believe that police misconduct occurred regularly (Dowler & Zawilski, 2007; Intravia et al., 2017).

With regard to the effects of troubling police behavior, several research find that television news programs commonly depicted the police as violent. Stories often portrayed police officers as having a tendency of resorting to excessive force which are primarily viewed as instigating – a factor which strongly reduces public approval of the police (Kaminski & Jefferis, 1998; Weitzer, 2002; Chermak et al., 2006; Fridkin et al., 2017).

In particular, high-profile cases of police violence, especially ones which are repeated often and also accompanied with visual footage, produced the most extremely negative opinions regarding officers and policing practices (Weitzer & Tuch, 2004; Fridkin et al., 2017; Gauthier & Graziano, 2018; Graziano, 2018). Additionally, whenever a particular frame dominates media coverage, repeated exposure to that frame will have a greater impact on the way audiences process information (Druckman, 2011), which explains why repeated stories about police brutality can spark outrage. Additionally, coverage of police brutality seems to dominate other competing frames when there are various news stories about crime (Fridkin et al., 2017) and tend to dominate the public discourse even when other stories about crime are present. What is especially troubling for law enforcement is that the effects of news media content on public opinion seem to be asymmetric. As found by Jaeyong Choi (2021), negative news content produces more disapproval of the police for viewers than positive content produces a positive influence of opinion.

This is precisely the social context under which most of our current research observations on Twitter are taking place. The American public, saturated by repeated visual content of police brutality in the death of George Floyd in Minneapolis, produced widespread outrage over policing in the United States, impacting the public debate about police reform theories and concepts. The public discourse which we studied, the framing of police reform among the public using Twitter, took place primarily within a context of anger and emotion – which we believe to have greatly obfuscated public understanding in terms of what constitute these various police reforms.

Social scientists have found that continuous media exposure to crime increases the salience of crime as a social problem for the public, leading to concerns about crime among viewers and demand of action from government leaders (Holbrook & Hill, 2005). This relationship between content frequency and public concern is known among media effects researchers as an "agenda-setting effect" (McCombs, 2014), where news coverage primes viewers toward increased levels of concern about issues being covered. The agenda-setting effect pertains to all potential social problems – including the social construction of police as being a social problem in itself – rather than as a solution to crime. Repeated and high-profile stories of police brutality, violence, corruption, incompetence, and as a dysfunctional institution in need of reform transform policing into a social problem rather than as a solution to the social problem of addressing crime and maintaining social order. It is within this understanding, where policing itself has become defined by the public as a social problem which urgently needs to be addressed, which serves as the contextual backdrop for our own research.

Fictional Media Coverage: Police and Crime

While most research of policing and media effects focuses on news coverage, Americans spend much more of their time viewing fictional media content. In contrast to television news broadcasts, fictional genres are consistently found by researchers to portray law enforcement very positively (Dowler, 2002; Surette 2007; Intravia et al., 2017), often defining the police as heroes who are highly effective at fighting crime. Programs often package police investigations as being extremely effective, nearly always catching the perpetrator quickly – nearly always making an arrest, never purposely targeting innocent people, and virtually always without error in the arrests being made (Dowler, 2002; Britto et al., 2007; Boda & Szabo, 2011; Donovan & Klahm, 2015). Additionally, the police are rarely shown to be corrupt, and when they engage in acts of violence, it is perceived as necessary to effectively do their job (Dowler, 2002; Leishman & Mason, 2003; Donovan & Klahm, 2015).

In fictional accounts of police violence, these acts generally take place within the context of being exercised against deeply nefarious characters who will not otherwise comply with police investigations (Eschholz et al., 2003; Donovan & Klahm, 2015). Offenders are often identified as psychopaths who are solely responsible for these crimes, rather than as actions that are situationally based, or draw from complex social contexts. These offenders are often depicted as being the instigators of violence with law enforcement as well – and that officers generally never purposely target innocent people (Donovan & Klahm, 2015).

Another common facet of fictional crime show genre is a highly overrepresentation of violent crimes and murder, with a lack of the more common petty offenses or victimless crimes police often investigate. In much of this content, it is purported that the police fearlessly and effectively protect the public from extremely dangerous people. These media accounts of police often construct a "good guys wear blue" framework (Donovan & Klahm, 2015) in the construction of relatively simplistic plotlines – where police do no wrong and are the thin blue line which protects the public from unspeakable acts of terror and violence.

As a result, audiences often form pro-police attitudes and beliefs. Research has found that a majority of viewers who watch at least one hour of crime dramas per week were more likely to believe that police are very successful in reducing crime, use the right amount of force, that this force is necessary, and it does not lead to flawed policing (Sacco, 1995; Surette, 2007; Boda & Szabo, 2011; Donovan & Klahm, 2015). These storylines, while distorting the reality of actual police work and compelling to viewers, have an ability to lead the public to positive and yet unrealistic expectations for law enforcement. In this context, heavy viewers of fictional media accounts, which are not counterbalanced by contrary information about crime (either actual or fictionalized), are susceptible to being overly optimistic about police practices and results.

Critics of these social constructions feel that these excessively positive depictions of police overlook significant concerns the public should hold about law enforcement. Many of the claimsmakers who oppose these representations of police act as a form of propaganda. A recent twist on this concept, one whose origins originate from Twitter protesters, is the notion of "Copaganda", viewed as any content which uncritically advances a police department's image or undermines reform efforts (Gallagher, 2020; Thomas, 2020). While the vast majority of this media content is produced by groups of people largely unaffiliated with law enforcement, producing content primarily as for-profit entertainment, critics interpret this content as endorsing dysfunctional policing. Although the creators generally never overtly endorse conservative political values or any specific social policy objectives, it is feared that the net effects of consuming these media messages serve the interests of the state and reinforces those accused of abusing power (Johnson, 2018; Grady, 2021).

In perhaps the most controversial example of Copaganda is the reality-based television show *Cops*, which aired for more than 30 years and produced more than 1,000 episodes. These episodes relied entirely on the video content of real-life calls which were narrated by police accounts of what they wanted audiences to know. The accounts from the show found the police nearly always aggressively capturing a suspect, who were often depicted with no backstory or empathy and often referred to by police as "the bad guys" (Molofsky, 2020). While being critiqued for its overly simplistic, one-sided positive portrayals of police officers as valorous, the content was also heavily edited by police departments themselves to constantly portray policing in a positive light – actively serving as a recruitment tool (Molofsky, 2020). The show, while being popular and highly profitable, was viewed by critics as an unethical handpicked distortion of reality that celebrated police aggression and violence as necessities of the job (Molofsky, 2020).

Police have also been criticized for intentionally distorting real-life policing in news reports as well. Critics have pointed to police-backed attempts to spin public opinion in their favor in news accounts, where the use of phrases like "officer-involved shooting" and officer "altercation" act as soft words that mask accounts of police violence. When interacting with journalists, law enforcement agencies have been accused of misrepresenting facts and purposely using artificial accounts through the release of biased public relation-based documents with reporters. Beyond the obscuring of facts, police departments have even been accused of actively engaging in smearing campaigns of victims to justify actions and avoid accountability (Johnson, 2018; Grady, 2021).

Regardless of whether Copaganda is a valid media effect or a rhetorical fear-based allegation against law enforcement, researchers are increasingly turning their attention to how and why police are finding value in taking their role as potential claimsmakers seriously. At nearly all levels of law enforcement institutions, there is a recognition that media messages matter in terms of public opinion and behavior, and managing media can serve their interests (Graziano, 2018). By using media to communicate effectively with the public, law enforcement can meet a variety of goals. These goals include voicing their own factual claims and perspective into public discourse, improving their status and credibility with the community, building community trust, and acting as an informational resource for solving crimes (Choi et al., 2020).

Policing Media Content: The Police as Claimsmakers

Journalists and fiction writers are not the only people who construct narratives of police actions or characters, and they do not have a monopoly on the production of media content that pertains to law enforcement. Police departments themselves also construct mass media content in efforts to better inform the public and to influence public opinion in directions which meet their own self-interests. Law enforcement agencies are becoming much more attentive to the tenor of the national news media, making more attempts to effectively communicate with public and to proactively get in front of stories so that official facts of the case are publicized before the public narrative might become skewed (Borcyk, 2020). For example, more agencies are training officers to perform their duties as if they are being recorded at all times. Additionally, many participants have stated in survey responses that their agency has upped their presence on social media platforms such as Facebook, Twitter, and Instagram (Borcyk, 2020).

Dating back to the television show *Dragnet*, which originally debuted in 1951, the modern-day cop show is viewed by some as emanating from a close relationship between Hollywood and the police (Grady, 2021), where writers rely on police to form believable accounts of police tactics, investigation practices, and daily routines. It is claimed that writers nearly always portrayed police positively and heroically and that even when shows depict officers acting less than admirable, scripts often connect such behavior to structural flaws in law enforcement rather than on corruption or self-conscious abuses of power. In their book *Cop Shows*, Sabin and colleagues (2015) discuss how a succession of "cop shows" over several decades, normalized public perceptions of police as predominantly moral, white, male heroes. Storyline conventions centered around savvy officers using their high level of problem-solving skills, which they often combined with a judicious use of force, to effectively preserve social order (Sabin et al., 2015).

A central motivation behind the increased role of police agencies desiring to influence public discourse has to do with protecting the professional image of police officers. Recent research has shown that law enforcement officers widely believe that no mediums in the United States portray them accurately or positively, as police officers predominantly view national news media to disproportionately depicting police in a negative light (Nix et al., 2019; Borcyk, 2020). Officers often express that their recorded actions are taken out of context, as reporters rely on broadcasting brief video clips, which do not accurately capture the event by ignoring crucial information of what happened in the preceding moments leading to the action being filmed (Borcyk, 2020).

This perception of unfair media representation reduces police morale and cooperation levels with the public, even leading some officers to second-guess their actions based on how they may be viewed by news media (Nix et al., 2019; Borcyk, 2020). Law enforcement officers feel that news coverage has made their work tougher (Morin et al., 2017), as the public perceives police as hostile – which includes hurting, or even killing – members of the public solely because officers are perceived to have an alleged power complex (Borcyk, 2020). In an interesting twist on media effects research, some claim that perceptions of unfair treatment and the propensity to depict the police as violent created a "Ferguson Effect". This term derives from news media depictions of police dealing with protestors in Ferguson, Missouri during 2014, after the death of Michael Brown at the hands of local police – when news footage primarily showed police as acting violently and aggressively with protesters.

This coverage, which produced widespread criticism of law enforcement from the public, is believed by some to directly create an increased amount of distancing of police from their communities, reducing their patrols and public visibility. This reduction of proactivity is hypothesized to be directly a result of officers feeling unappreciated and villainized by the communities they serve (Nix & Wolfe, 2015; Nix & Wolfe, 2016; Nix et al., 2019). Depictions of police activities such as these, which were largely formed outside of police accounts and narratives of these events, have served as motivation for law enforcement to actively embrace the role of claimsmakers (Best, 2016).

However, as mentioned earlier, police as claimsmakers does invite the potential for a conflict of interest, as there can be self-interested reasons for law enforcement to purposely misinform the public. Some have questioned the degree to which media content originated by police are valid and trustworthy accounts that the public should believe. While law enforcement holds the legal right to inform the public, make claims, and defend themselves from the accusations of other claimsmakers, there is concern for the potential damaging of public discourse.

A Cloudy Picture: Mass Media Content and Public Perceptions of the Police

Ultimately, what people see and hear about the police in modern mass media is a constant stream of negative and positive messages simultaneously coexisting with one another in a variety of mediums each day. Overall, there is no clear consensus regarding how the police are portrayed in the media (Dowler, 2002; Intravia et al., 2017; Choi et al., 2020) – as media content of police continually offer both positive and negative depictions, with mixed results on the attitudes of audiences. Of course, what further complicates the relationship between the viewing of media content and audiences is the fact that these audiences are overlapping – that virtually all mass media viewers consume a mixture of fictional and nonfictional content. The nearly endless amount of media content being produced and consumed each day in movies, television shows, and news broadcasts paints a very mixed picture about policing in the United States. Given the massive amount of media content the average American consumes each day, it may be no surprise that the public develops highly ambivalent opinions about the police. Research indicates that our age, racial identity, living environment, personal experiences with police officers, and the types of mass media consumption we engage in interact in highly complex ways, making inconsistent impressions on our beliefs and attitudes about policing.

In a social world where people are more likely to form beliefs about the police through vicarious experiences via mediated content rather than personal experience, it seems clear that representations of policing are of dire importance. How people think about the police impacts public support for law enforcement and what types of policy they support. By studying what people tweet about how they feel about law enforcement practices, we hope to discover what the American public feel on this topic – in their own words. The remainder of this book focuses exclusively on what Americans tweeted during a time of crisis in the public's trust in law enforcement. Through content analysis of tweets, we aim to identify what people believe about the police, their understanding of what reform options are available, the types of reform they support or oppose, and beliefs about whether the public views these ideas as promising or not.

References

Altheide, D. L. (2015). *The media syndrome*. Routledge Press.

Berger, P. L., & Luckmann, T. (1966). *The social construction of reality: A treatise in the sociology of knowledge*. Anchor Books.

Berry, J. M., & Sobieraj, S. (2016). *The outrage industry: Political opinion media and the new Incivility*. Oxford University Press.

Best, J. (2016). *Social problems* (3rd ed.). WW Norton & Company.

Boda, Z., & Szabo, G. (2011). The media and attitudes towards crime and the justice system: A qualitative approach. *European Journal of Criminology, 8*(4), 329–342.

Borcyk, A. (2020). *Law enforcement, public opinion, the media, and its effects* [Theses/Capstones/Creative Projects, University of Nebraska at Omaha]. https://digitalcom mons.unomaha.edu/university_honors_program/89

Britto, S., Hughes, T., Saltzman, K., & Stroh, C. (2007). Does special mean young, white and female? Deconstructing the meaning of 'special' in 'Law & Order: Special Victims Unit.' *Journal of Criminal Justice and Popular Culture, 14*(1), 39–57.

Callanan, V. J., & Rosenberger, J. S. (2011). Media and public perceptions of the police: Examining the impact of race and personal experience. *Policing and Society*, *21*(2), 167–189.

Chermak, S., McGarrell, E., & Gruenewald, J. (2006). Media coverage of police misconduct and attitudes toward police. *Policing: An International Journal of Police Strategies and Management*, *29*(2), 261-281.

Chiricos, T., Eschholz, S., & Gertz, M. (1997). Crime, news, and fear of crime: Toward an identification of audience effects. *Social Problems*, *44*(3), 342–357.

Chiricos, T., Padgett, K., & Gertz, M. (2000). Fear, TV news, and the reality of crime. *Criminology*, *38*(3), 755–786.

Choi, J. (2021). Asymmetry in media effects on perceptions of police: An analysis using a within-subjects design experiment, *Police Practice and Research*, *22*(1), 557–573.

Choi, J., Kim, H., & Hicks, R. D. (2020). Direct and indirect effects of crime-related media consumption on public confidence in police. *International Journal of Police Science & Management*, *22*(1), 38–49.

Colbran, M. (2014). *Media representations of police and crime: Shaping the police television drama*. Palgrave Macmillan.

Custers, K., & Van den Bulck, J. (2013). The cultivation of fear of sexual violence in women: Processes and moderators of the relationship between television and fear. *Communication Research*, *40*(1), 96–124.

Donovan K. M., & Klahm, I. C. F. (2015). The role of entertainment media in perceptions of police use of force. *Criminal Justice and Behavior*, *42*(12), 1261–1281.

Dowler, K. (2002). Media consumption and public attitudes toward crime and justice: The relationship between fear of crime, punitive attitudes, and perceived police effectiveness. *Journal of Criminal Justice and Popular Culture*, *10*(2), 109–126.

Dowler, K., & Zawilski, V. (2007). Public perceptions of police misconduct and discrimination: Examining the impact of media consumption. *Journal of Criminal Justice*, *35*(2), 193–203.

Downie Jr., L., & Kaiser, R. G. (2003). *The news about the news: American journalism in peril*. Vintage Books.

Druckman, J. N. (2011). What's it all about? Framing in political science. In G. Keren (Ed.), *Perspectives on framing* (pp. 279-302). Psychology Press.

Dunaway, J. L., & Graber, D. (2022). *Mass media & American politics* (11th ed.). CQ Press.

Eith, C., & Durose, M. R. (2011). *Contacts between police and the public, 2008*. (NCJ 234599). U.S. Department of Justice, Bureau of Justice Statistics.

Eschholz, S., Mallard, M., & Flynn, S. (2003). Images of primetime justice: A content analysis of 'NYPD Blue' and 'Law & Order.' *Journal of Criminal Justice and Popular Culture*, *10*(3), 161–180.

Fridkin, K., Wintersieck, A., Courey, J., & Thompson, J. (2017). Race and police brutality: The importance of media framing. *International Journal of Communication*, *11*, 3394–3414.

Gallagher, B. (2020, February 28). Just say no to viral 'copaganda' videos. *Daily Dot*. www.dailydot.com/irl/cop-viral-videos/

Gauthier, J. F., & Graziano, L. (2018). News media consumption & attitudes about police: In search of theoretical orientation and advancement. *Journal of Crime & Justice*, *41*(5), 504–520.

Gerbner, G. (1993). Society's storyteller: How TV creates the myths by which we live. *Center for Media Literacy*. www.medialit.org/reading-room/societys-storyteller-how-tv-creates-myths-which-we-live

Gerbner, G., & Gross, L. (1976). Living with television: The violence profile. *Journal of Communication*, *26*(2), 172–194.

Gerbner, G., Gross, L., Jackson-Beeck, M., Jeffries-Fox, S., & Signorielli, N. (1978). Cultural indicators: Violence profile no. 9. *Journal of Communication*, *28*(3), 176–207.

Gerbner, G., Gross, L., Morgan, G., & Signorielli, N. (1986). Living with television: The dynamics of the cultivation process. In J. Bryant & D. Zillman (Eds.), *Perspectives on media effects* (pp. 17–40). Erlbaum.

Gerbner, G., Gross, L., Morgan, M., & Signorielli, N. (1980). The "mainstreaming" of America: Violence profile no. 11. *Journal of Communication*, *30*(3), 10–29.

Gilliam, F. D., & Iyengar, S. (2000). Prime suspects: The influence of local television news on the viewing public. *American Journal of Political Science*, *44*(3), 560–573.

Grady, C. (2021, April 12). How 70 years of cop shows taught us to valorize the police. *Vox Magazine*. www.vox.com/culture/22375412/police-show-procedurals-hollywood-history-dragnet-keystone-cops-brooklyn-nine-nine-the-wire-blue-bloods

Graziano, L. (2018), News media and perceptions of police: A state-of-the-art review. *Policing: An International Journal*, *42*(2), 209–225.

Hinds, L., & Murphy, K. (2007). Public satisfaction with police: Using procedural justice to improve police legitimacy. *Australian & New Zealand Journal of Criminology*, *40*(1), 27–42.

Holbrook, R. A., & Hill, T. G. (2005). Agenda-setting and priming in prime time television: Crime dramas as political cues. *Political Communication*, *22*(3), 277–295.

Intravia, J., Wolff, K. T., & Piquero, A. R. (2017). Investigating the effects of media consumption on attitudes toward police legitimacy. *Deviant Behavior*, *39*(8), 963–980.

Iyengar, S., & Kinder, D. R. (2010). *News that matters: Television and American opinion* (Updated ed.). University of Chicago Press.

Jackson, J. B., Hohl, B. K., & Farrall. S. (2009). Does the fear of crime erode public confidence in policing? *Policing: A Journal of Policy and Practice*, *3*(1), 100–111.

Jackson, J. B., & Sunshine, J. (2007). Public confidence in policing: A neo-Durkheimian perspective. *British Journal of Criminology*, *47*(2), 214–233.

Johnson, A. (2018, January 30). 6 elements of police spin: An objective lesson in copspeak. *Fairness & Accuracy in Reporting*. https://fair.org/home/6-elements-of-police-spin-an-object-lesson-in-copspeak/

Jones, J. M. (2022, July 5). Confidence in U.S. institutions down; Average at a new low. *Gallup*. https://news.gallup.com/poll/394283/confidence-institutions-down-average-new-low.aspx

Kaminski, R. J., & Jefferis, E. S. (1998). The effect of a violent televised arrest on public perceptions of the police: A partial test of Easton's theoretical framework. *Policing: An International Journal of Police Strategies and Management*, *21*(4), 683–706.

Klapper, J. T. (1960). *The effects of mass communication*. Free Press.

Langton, L., & Durose, M. (2013). *Police behavior during traffic and street stops, 2011*. U.S. Department of Justice, Office of Justice Programs, & Bureau of Justice Statistics.

Leishman, F., & Mason, P. (2003). *Policing and the media: Facts, fictions, and factions*. Willan Publishing.

Lippmann, W. (2020). *Public opinion*. DigiReads Publishing.

McCall, J. M. (2007). *Viewer discretion advised: Taking control of mass media influences*. Rowman & Littlefield.

McCombs, M. (2014). *Setting the agenda* (2nd ed.). Polity Press.

McCombs, M., Holbert, R. L., Kiousis, S., & Wanta, W. (2011). *The news and public opinion: Media effects on civic life*. Polity Press.

Molofsky, H. (2020, June 11). Cops: The violent legacy of a TV show that sculpted America's view of police. *The Guardian*. www.theguardian.com/tv-and-radio/2020/jun/11/cops-american-police-tv-show

Morin, R., Parker, K., Stepler, R., & Mercer, A. (2017, January 11). Police views, public views. *Pew Research Center*. www.pewresearch.org/social-trends/2017/01/11/police-views-public-views/

Nix, J., Pickett, J. T., & Wolfe, S. E. (2019). Testing a theoretical model of perceived audience legitimacy: The neglected linkage in the dialogic model of police-community relations. *Journal of Research in Crime and Delinquency*, *57*(2), 217–259.

Nix, J., & Wolfe, S. E. (2015). The impact of negative publicity on police self-legitimacy. *Justice Quarterly*, *34*(1), 84–108.

Nix, J., & Wolfe, S. E. (2016). Sensitivity to the Ferguson effect: The role of managerial organizational justice. *Journal of Criminal Justice*, *47*, 12–20.

Roche, S. P., Pickett, J. T., & Gertz, M. (2016). The scary world of online news? Internet news exposure and public attitudes toward crime and justice. *Journal of Quantitative Criminology*, *32*(2), 215–236.

Rosenberg, H. (2009). *No time to think: The menace of media speed and the 24-hour news cycle*. Continuum Publishing.

Sabin, R., Wilson, R., Speidel, L., Faucette, B., & Bethell, B. (2015). *Cop shows: A history of police dramas on television*. McFarland & Company.

Sacco, V. (1995). Media constructions of crime. *Annals of the American Academy of Political and Social Science*, *539*, 141–154.

Schudson, M. (2011). *The sociology of news* (2nd ed.). W.W. Norton.

Shearer, E., & Matsa, K. E. (2018). News use across social media platforms 2018. *Pew Research Center*. www.pewresearch.org/journalism/2018/09/10/news-use-across-social-media-platforms-2018/

Skogan, W. G. (2009). Concern about crime and confidence in the police: Reassurance of accountability? *Police Quarterly, 12*(3), 301–318.

Stryker, S. (1980). *Symbolic interactionism: A social structural version.* Blackburn Press.

Surette, R. (2007). *Media, crime, and criminal justice* (2nd ed.). Wadsworth Publishing.

Surette, R. (2015). *Media, crime, and criminal justice: Images, realities, and policies.* Thomas Wadsworth Publishing.

Taibbi, M. (2020). *Hate, Inc: Why today's media makes us despise one another.* OR Books.

Thomas, A. R. (2020, June 8). Is TV finally done with "heroic" cops? A black showrunner says "hell f*cking no. *Vanity Fair.* www.vanityfair.com/hollywood/2020/06/tv-and-cops

Tuch, S. A., & Weitzer, R. 1997. Trends: Racial differences in attitudes toward the police. *Public Opinion Quarterly, 61*(4), 642-663.

Tyler, T. R. (2004). Enhancing police legitimacy. *The Annals of the American Academy of Political and Social Science, 593*(1), 84–99.

U.S. Bureau of Labor Statistics. (2015). *American time use survey – 2015 results.* www.bls.gov/news.release/archives/atus_06242016.pdf

U.S. Bureau of Labor Statistics. (2021). Occupational employment and wage statistics – police and sheriff's patrol officers. www.bls.gov/oes/current/oes333051.htm

Van Craen, M. (2013). Explaining majority and minority trust in the police. *Justice Quarterly, 30*(6), 1042–1067.

Weitzer, R. (2002). Incidents of police misconduct and public opinion. *Journal of Criminal Justice, 30*(5), 397-408.

Weitzer, R., & Kubrin, C. E. (2004). Breaking news: How local TV news and real-world conditions affect fear of crime. *Justice Quarterly, 21*(3), 497–520.

Weitzer, R., & Tuch, S. A. (1999). Race, class, and perceptions of discrimination by the police. *NCCD News, 45*(4), 494–507.

Weitzer, R., & Tuch, S. A. (2004). Race and perceptions of police misconduct. *Social Problems, 51*(3), 305–325.

Wu, Y. (2014). Race/ethnicity and perceptions of the police: A comparison of White, Black, Asian and Hispanic Americans. *Policing and Society, 24*(2), 135–157.

2

ABOLISH THE POLICE ON TWITTER

Introduction

During the summer of 2020, the United States experienced extreme tension and social crisis related to race and policing, mainly stemming from the video recorded death of George Floyd at the hands of Minneapolis police – images which caused outrage all around the world. In the ensuing weeks, nationwide protests emerged across the United States in support of the Black Lives Matter movement. During this time period, a large percentage of the public expressed opposition to police violence, launching a national dialogue about this continuing problem. One concept which surfaced during this process involved the idea of abolishing the police – an idea which has existed among academic researchers for years but is still a relatively new and largely unexplored concept among the general public.

In this chapter, we review what abolish the police means among academic writers, but also explore how everyday people are discussing the concept on Twitter. How does the public understand this concept, and how does this conceptualization vary from the understanding held among academic writers? Additionally, our goal is to describe why these Twitter users want to abolish the police, and how discourse of this topic is often subdivided by differing focus areas among various authors. Via the collection and observation of 500 tweets using the hashtag *#AbolishThePolice*, we are able to describe some frameworks constructed by the public.

Abolish the Police – Definition and Origins

The term "abolish the police" is an idea that has existed for decades within academic and activist circles. It originated in the social activist beliefs of Angela Davis and Ruth Wilson Gilmore before quickly leaping into public conscience during the summer of 2020 (Arietta-Kenna, 2020). While various thinkers and activists view the phrase as a serious call to rethink the very concept of law enforcement in the United States, there is still not a consensus agreement on the meaning of "abolish the police" (Illing, 2020). Instead, this phrase has multivalent meanings, depending on which group is using the slogan (Arietta-Kenna, 2020). For example, a person can think of it as a literal policy proposal, or instead, it can be used as a rhetorical device designed to shift the paradigm on what is

DOI: 10.4324/9781003224440-2

politically feasible as a way of encouraging readers to become imaginative about potential reforms to policing and law enforcement. While the former supports the idea of fully eliminating the police in the United States, the latter purports that the actual goal of the movement is *not* to terminate the police. Instead, the goal is to frame the discussion in a way that makes radical change plausible (Illing, 2020).

However, in virtually all forms of use, the terminology offers some unsettling insights about the origins and history of American policing (Arietta-Kenna, 2020). In general, those who employ the use of "Abolish the Police" often identify American police as being rooted in racism and white supremacy and view the police as excessively violent. Beyond this point, there is also divergence between writers who believe the institution can be reformed versus those who view policing in the United States as terminally toxic, abusive, and wholly beyond reform.

Abolish as Defined in the Most Literal Sense: No More Police

The most extreme meaning construction of "abolish the police" is the most literal interpretation – one in which the phrase means precisely what it says. Within this conceptualization, writers do not mean reimagining or reinventing the police force, but instead espouse the literal end of the institution of policing in the United States (Arietta-Kenna, 2020). Under this interpretation, police abolition is predicated on the idea that police are predominantly harmful to people and must be abolished. Abolitionists push back against the ideas of reformists, insisting that police reform will lead to more unnecessary criminalization and police-instigated violence in their communities (Correia & Wall, 2017). These justifications for ending police forces in the United States rely on two factors. The first involves *a definition of the institution rooted in white supremacy*, which is designed to use state-sanctioned violence to deprive non-whites of liberty, with the second being *the belief that American policing, as a system, is inherently flawed and beyond reformation*.

As stated earlier, *abolitionists often view the institution as rooted in white supremacy, designed to use state-sanctioned violence to deprive non-whites of liberty*. Those who support this viewpoint refer to history, citing that today's police forces were originally formed by slave owners. In that system, volunteer citizens acted as slave patrols on plantations, using violence and intimidation to control black Americans. This system was based on exerting power and control over black lives, having little to do with crime control (Jones-Brown & King-Toler, 2011; Spruill, 2016; Kappeler & Gaines, 2012). These writers view our current police structure as a continuation of institutionally sanctioned violent practices and imprisonment as instruments of control over the lives of black Americans today (Arietta-Kenna, 2020). Such practices are viewed as purposely keeping black people poor and powerless in the same manner in which policing was originally designed for: to purposely maintain a status quo of white racial dominance in American society.

As a result, modern police organizations in the United States are still viewed as having ideological attachments to these early slave patrols, accused of viewing black Americans as not fully human. Abolitionists view police as a force that protects wealthy white property owners by suppressing the rights of lower classes via targeting the poor. Police are thought of as prison-industrial complex foot soldiers, with practices that incentivize and reward officers for maximizing their presence in people's lives. Additionally, police departments are accused of arresting citizens solely for profit incentives, selling "vulnerable people" to prisons to fill their beds in a for-profit system (Purnell, 2017; Briond, 2020).

In particular, there is deep concern over the propensity for violence and police aggression toward black Americans (Vitale, 2017; Purnell, 2017; Arietta-Kenna, 2020; Illing, 2020). Abolitionists claim that relying on police benevolence leaves black people vulnerable to the arbitrary spectrum of police violence (Purnell, 2017; Vitale & Casleton, 2020), as demonstrated by black people being disproportionately stopped, shot, and killed by police (Arietta-Kenna, 2020; DeGue et al., 2016; Gaston, 2019; Koch et al., 2016; Carbado, 2017; Bleich et al., 2019; Bergman, 2018). As a result, there are very high levels of tension, mutual distrust, and a fear of violence between police and urban communities, producing a "Warrior mentality"[1] among police officers working in urban areas (Vitale, 2017). This in turn increases anxiety and a fear of violence for both police officers and black Americans, viewed as causing police to increasingly respond to perceived threats with violence. To combat this perceived threat, police have become more militarized, decreasing civility levels, empathy, and humanity between officers and the public in urban areas. Such actions have fueled the calls for police abolition (Vitale, 2017).

Also, there exists *the sustained belief that American policing, as a system, is inherently flawed and cannot be reformed*. A central tenant among abolitionists is that police forces cannot effectively be reformed and point out that previous attempts to make incremental institutional policy changes to policing have failed to achieve their goals. There is a belief that any reformist reform approach to American policing will always fail (McDowell & Fernandez, 2018) by asking the question "how can we re-center an entity as a public good if it never was one?" (Purnell, 2017, para. 3).

For abolitionists adopting this variant in the definition of the term, the death of George Floyd both confirmed and intensified their beliefs that the police are simply unfixable. For example, the Minneapolis Police Department have tried to reform itself many times before: implementing implicit-bias training, creating use-of-force standards, and adopting body cameras for officers, but officers such as Derek Chauvin still routinely commit violence (Arietta-Kenna, 2020). As Isaac Bryan[2] states, "We are past the point of superficial reforms that do little to change the material conditions for those who have disproportionate, and often lethal, contact with law enforcement" (Illing, 2020, para. 48). Overall, there is a lot of pessimism regarding the likelihood of effective reform. According to Jen Jackson:[3]

> Reforms do not work . . . police have had already undergone extensive anti-bias training, receiving body cameras, and engaged in other reformist options for reducing police violence, such as banning chokeholds . . . these [reforms] are not proven methods. They are just digestible for white Americans who still believe that police protect and serve indiscriminately.
>
> *(Illing, 2020, para. 29)*

Alex Vitale (2017) supports such claims, stating that increased racial diversity among police forces and more sensitivity training programs have had no effect on policing. Instead, institutional pressures have continually encouraged the use of excessive force in dealing with the public while simultaneously discouraging transparency and accountability to the public. Thus, while reformists are seeking to address ways in which policing can be conducted more humanely and effectively, abolitionists wish to eliminate its practice altogether through a process of disbanding, disempowering, and disarming the police (McDowell & Fernandez, 2018).

Recently, there have been some non-abolitionists who have voiced their support for the "#8CantWait" movement. This approach calls for eight specific, direct, concrete, and immediately implementable reforms to improving policing. The specific reforms include banning chokeholds, emphasizing de-escalation techniques, requiring a verbal warning before shooting, using shooting as a last resort, banning shooting at moving vehicles, requiring comprehensive reporting, limiting the use of weapons, and requiring officer intervention into the use of excessive force (Yglesias, 2020a). However, those within the abolitionist framework largely reject these notions as unproductive "incrementalism" (@HCYDSA), which protects police by suggesting that real reform can be accomplished internally through moderate measures. Skeptics, such as Christian Davenport,[4] note that "it is also not really clear where these policy prescriptions come from and why we would think they would work" (Illing, 2020, para. 32).

Nevertheless, the concept of reform causes some disruption in the meaning of abolishing the police, as some believe that police departments can be reformed. As a result, there are some whose use of the word "abolish" acts as a rhetorical strategy for its users to employ to aggressively pursue change. Abolish essentially "acts as a bargaining chip" or a way to urge basic, more popular police reforms by employing a classic activist technique push for a maximalist idea and then meet in the middle (Arietta-Kenna, 2020, para. 7).

Abolish the Police Is Sometimes Used as a Call for Reform

Perhaps, the largest disconnect among users of #AbolishThePolice is defining what role police reform plays in the movement. As previously discussed, some take the most extreme definition of "abolish" and wish to eliminate police forces entirely. However, others identify "abolish" as a call for reform. They may use the phrase or utilize the hashtag as "an excellent choice of those who have been trying for years to prompt a national conversation about police" (Arietta-Kenna, 2020, para. 9). Moreover, "abolish the police" is depicted as an objective goal to rally behind, inviting the opportunity to completely rethink how police departments in the United States are funded and to clarify what laws are meant to govern them (VanDerWerff, 2020).

Reformists also criticize the more idealistic abolition voices as unrealistic and naïve, rejecting the notion that society can function without a professional police force. They view a statement such as "abolish the police" not as a singular and literal solution but as a pragmatic attempt to achieve meaningful changes in policing. While police are viewed as problematic and in need of enormous change, a full abolition is viewed as being a step too far, arguing that "even the most hardcore advocate of this position would agree that we should probably have a process for dealing with murder and other violent crimes" (VanDerWerff, 2020, para. 13). With respect to how police reform can be achieved, there are two specific approaches which are most commonly voiced: (1) rethinking the duties and responsibilities of police, coupled with police defunding and (2) reinventing policing by requiring communities to create policing alternatives.

Abolish as Rethinking the Duties and Responsibilities of Police, Coupled With Defunding

The terminology of abolishing the police is often used as a redistribution call for both public services and taxpayer funding. The root of the problem, from this perspective, is the dramatic expansion of police roles over the last 40 years. This expansion is viewed as being inconsistent with community empowerment, social justice, and even public safety. Thus, it is argued that there is a dire need for increased investments in other community resources, in conjunction with a decriminalization of practices like drug use, prostitution, homelessness, and border patrolling, among other things (Vitale, 2017). In turn, communities need more health professionals or social workers to be trained as first responders to nonviolent situations, as well as employing unarmed mediation and interruption teams that are equipped to prevent violence-first responses (Arietta-Kenna, 2020). By redefining police boundaries:

We have learned that reforming police agencies and changing laws is necessary, but not sufficient. To fix policing, we have to recognize that, as police themselves have been telling us for years, they are doing too much . . . there are some things that police are doing that nobody should be doing, such as enforcing laws that criminalize poverty and addition, arresting people instead of issuing citations, writing tickets to raise revenue rather than protect the public, and using armored vehicles to evict people from a home they have occupied to protest homelessness.[5]

(Illing, 2020, para. 34)

It follows that defunding police departments serves the practical goal of freeing up money for other local services that might help to reduce crime in a community over the long term, such as mental health treatment, drug rehabilitation, poverty relief, education, and housing (Arietta-Kenna, 2020; Boyum et al., 2011; Pullmann, 2011; Cuellar et al., 2006; Frank & McGuire, 2011; Chandler et al., 2009; Bondurant et al., 2018; Palmer et al., 2019; Liebertz & Bunch, 2018; Lochner, 2020; Rudolph & Starke, 2020).

We need to scrutinize our state and local budgets, education ourselves about what police do versus what we need to be and feel safe, and realign the budget and cut out social programs to better serve our public safety needs. Much of what police do could probably be done better or more cost-effectively if done by somebody else: everything from taking accident reports to responding to persons who are homeless or in mental health crisis.[6]

(Illing, 2020, para. 16)

Reinventing the role of police departments shifts the conversation toward the expansion of other social services, which would ultimately be financed by defunding the police. This conception of defunding is framed as an "opportunity cost", where each dollar currently spent on policing is framed as money that is being stripped away from various other crucial but currently badly underfunded programs. By using funds currently allocated to police forces and reinvesting that money into community initiatives intended to reduce crime, the need for police forces resembling what we see today would not be necessary in the future. According to Bryan, "Now is the time to push further in the political discourse, divest from harm, and invest in opportunity" (Illing, 2020, para. 48). In doing so, added Christy Lopez, "we may find some law enforcement agencies are duplicative and don't need to exist" (Illing, 2020, para. 22).

Reinventing Policing and Requiring Communities to Create Policing Alternatives

This perspective centers around specifically identifying creative and practical versions of police reform. The basic premise is that the public still needs police forces and also that policing as we know it is so broken that departments cannot simply be reformed. Instead, reform requires scrapping our current police forces to allow a newer, better version to emerge, one that is more just and humane (Vitale, 2017; Arietta-Kenna, 2020). This is a slow, long-term process rather than a single event and is often viewed as a hybrid approach between the abolition and reform movements. With regard to the former, it calls for the firing of all existing police officers. Meanwhile, with respect to the latter, it also involves replacing all of the current police officers with new ones. This newly constructed police force would be much smaller, largely unarmed, and not trained in militaristic approaches to policing (Vitale, 2017).

Those working within this paradigm view police as beyond reform but break from the notions that police officers are fundamentally incapable of being something other than abusive pawns that serve the ruling elite. Instead, there is an insistence that there is a need for a functioning police force – just one that is largely unarmed and smaller. This approach involves a systematic questioning of what specific roles that police should be undertaking and attempting to develop evidence-based alternatives that will reduce the public's reliance on the police (Vitale, 2017). The new police force would be much smaller, largely unarmed, and not trained in militaristic approaches to policing (Vitale, 2017). Additionally, the scope of police work becomes greatly decreased through decriminalization, in conjunction with the expansion of other community-based responders, such as social workers.

Supporters of this approach claim that is has an established track record, pointing to this as evidence of success. In Camden, New Jersey, all of their police officers were fired in 2013, and a new police force was developed with different rules being outlined under the county government. The essential roles of the new police force were reframed to be community-oriented and to purposely focus on de-escalating violence. The city also reallocated funds toward community-building initiatives. Over the next few years, crime statistics for Camden indicated that crime rates had dropped, as did accusations of police violence and corruption (Arietta-Kenna, 2020; Langergan, 2020; Perry, 2020).

With this literature review in mind, we moved on to collect 500 tweets containing the hashtag *#AbolishThePolice* which were posted to Twitter between June 1 and June 10, 2020. As stated earlier, we used a combination of manifest and latent coding techniques to deconstruct the various meanings of how this concept was understood, discussed, and shared on Twitter by the public. Our central research question was to identify and illustrate "what does the public associate with the concept of abolishing the police?"

Findings

A quick summary of the manifest coding results can be seen in Table 2.1. Here we observed that two out of three writers in our sample evaluated the police negatively in their tweets. There was a significant amount of pessimism regarding police reform, where hashtag users believed by a more than a 4-to-1 ratio that the police cannot be reformed.

Our quantitative data findings indicated that 120 writers had exhibited anger in their tweets while 104 accused the police of racism, and 198 discussed police violence. These three characteristics were the most common traits found in our sample, leading us to delve deeper into how these themes were further elucidated by these authors. In the following descriptive section, we used latent coding to identify and describe content found within various unique frames that were found when referring to the *#AbolishThePolice* hashtag.

Tweets About Police Violence

As previously discussed, violence was the most recognized topic among those using the *#AbolishThePolice* hashtag. There was a widespread impression among writers that this violence was excessive and reflected an antipathy for people of color. A common opinion was that the police did not care about the public – that they "pretend to care about communities they serve" (@BenIuliano), which was a recurring theme found in our sample, where police are seen as having a general disinterest in community well-being. Moreover, the police were viewed predominantly as a "Militaristic, violent

TABLE 2.1 Summary of Manifest Coding

Description	Results From Sample: Frequency (%)
Does writer exhibit anger toward police?	Yes: 120 (23.9)
	No: 380 (76.1)
How does writer evaluate the police?	Negatively: 338 (67.2)
	Neutrally: 145 (28.8)
	Positively: 17 (3.4)
Are police accused of being racist?	Yes: 104 (20.7)
	No: 396 (79.3)
Does author believe police can be reformed?	Yes: 32 (6.4)
	Not answered: 321 (63.8)
	No: 147 (29.2)
Are police accused/shown as being violent?	Yes: 198 (39.4)
	No: 302 (60.6)

system that must be torn down" (@meg_lo_maniacal), and "A force trained for occupation and oppression" (@thecrisismag). As one writer stated, #Abolish means "Defund, Demilitarize, and Dissolve the Police force. They do not serve the people" (@jcruzLA).

Frameworks of "#AbolishThePolice" Found on Twitter

The remainder of this chapter will provide the readers with a detailed examination of how these frameworks were constructed, often using direct quotes to illustrate central claims, as well as exploring assumptions, which were made by these authors.

After careful analysis of these tweets, we identified six key frameworks that emerged. We have given these frames the following titles, with a brief summary of common themes and assumptions most often found within these frameworks given in a bullet-points format:

1. "All Cops Are Bastards"

- Police officers are believed to consistently abuse power in their own self-interests.
- Police officers are viewed as being unaccountable for their actions.
- Police officers are said to personally enjoy violence.

2. "Hyperviolent Policing"

- Police officers are depicted as lacking a sense of decency.
- Police are commonly associated with murderers and terrorists.
- Police are perceived as perpetrating violence, consistently acting as aggressors.

3. "Slave Patrol"

- Modern policing is said to be rooted in racism, dating back to the control of slaves.
- Policing in the United States has always purposely served the interest of whites through the intentional oppression of racial minorities.
- American policing, due to its inherently racialized past, is incapable of reform.

4. "Reform Rejection"

- Police have a long history of successfully being able to avoid accountability and reform efforts in the United States.
- Police departments are insulated from reform efforts by other social institutions, such as by government officials.
- There is a pro-police sentiment in mass media, which acts to reduce the public's demand for police reform.

5. "We Keep Us Safe"

- The need for professional police officers is openly questioned, with a call for citizen patrols to replace the current police.
- Police are said to be ineffective at either preventing crime or catching criminals.

6. "Opportunity Cost"

- Monies invested into police budgets reduce spending on other crucially needed community programs.
- Reducing the size and scope of policing would be beneficial to communities.

#Abolish and Abuse of Power: The "All Cops Are Bastards" Frame

Police officers were often viewed as self-serving people who will abuse power to do whatever they feel like while unethically protecting themselves, and each other, from any accountability (@egypt-ncowboy). Writers accused the police of being callous individuals who are criminals themselves. About 30 times, writers used the hashtag "#ACAB", which stands for "all cops are bastards" – referring to the mindset of abusing power with impunity. One writer describes further by saying, "They are not serving us, and they only protect themselves" (@bfister) while another adds that the police "believe they are above the law because they are" (@tehlorkay).

A number of posts featured some egregious examples that showed officers abusing their powers. One such post included a TikTok video of a police officer talking about how much he enjoys police brutality (@caffeine_adct) while another included a retweeted article about a former cop who confesses that he "was a bastard", and added that "we all were" (@Arvlol). The article goes on to describe a common workday of believing the law does not apply to you and a mindset that violence was always accepted as a part of your work. A couple of other retweeted stories included one where an officer on Facebook threatened a restaurant owner who stopped offering him free food (@browofjustice) and another involving two San Diego police officers who were captured on video threatening a café worker for wearing a #BLM face mask at work (@danarel).

During protests in June 2020, the police were depicted as assaulting protesters "with wild abandon" (@ewsorg) while using excessive force "every chance they get" (@djskeez313). One writer added that the protest they were attending was peaceful primarily "because the police were not there" (@JonSiebels). The following are some of the other tweets we viewed:

A retweeted story about how NYPD was working with ICE to detain protesters which they know are American citizens as a form of harassment and brutality.

(@whitney_hu)

A claim that "Cops regularly retaliate against anyone who tries to hold them accountable. They're nothing but state-sanctioned mobsters".

(@radicalbytes)

A woman who was nearly run over by a motorcycle cop who ran a red light in New York City because he "just didn't feel like stopping".

(@ClaireMPLS)

Likewise, 26 videos were posted on Twitter during this time period in which police officers were filmed acting violently toward unarmed individuals at protests, such as claims that Louisville police officers had turned off their body cameras to hide their violence against protesters on June 1. Similar accusations of police circumventing accountability, while also being excessively violent, were made throughout the nation among the tweets observed in this sample.

#Abolish and Police Violence: The "Hyperviolent Policing" Frame

Within this narrative, police officers are accused of actually enjoying the excessive use of violence at every opportunity, which were said to motivate them toward this career in the first place. Many referred to police officers as state-sponsored terrorists and accused them of being murderers. While many connected violence to a lack of accountability for their actions, others felt that police officers genuinely enjoy being violent and were people who lack empathy or decency. One writer tweeted that police inherently have "a psychological need for full control over others" (@CatboyPsyop) while another writer retweeted a news story about cops being prone to domestic violence at home (@designmom). In general, police officers were routinely viewed as "continually injuring and murdering people", and abolishing police was viewed as the "only way things will change" (@muted_goat). Another writer added that "police have brutalized and murdered us every chance that they've ever gotten" (@lilithxsinclair). This was best exemplified in a widely circulated photo during this time period, an elderly unarmed protester in Buffalo, New York, was injured by riot police, who then deny finding him medical care as they continue to march toward protesters. This visual image was often tweeted and retweeted as an example of how violent and inhumane police officers acted toward the public (@MikiTakesPhotos).

Within this subgroup of postings about violence, the police were identified as either "murderers" or "terrorists" a total of 38 times. The perceived lack of humanity among the police produced the following list of quotes:

"They want to KILL innocent lives! This is NOT okay!"

(@jfalahess)

"Won't even stop killing when you burn their shit down".

(@dreadpiratejene)

Police "constantly get away with murdering black people" (@jaeandthecity) and are claimed to be "Perpetrators of violence that assassinate black lives".

(@tamikahs66)

The filming of police violence was widely circulated on Twitter from June 1 to June 10. The use of tear gas and police brutality against crowds was shown dozens of times. Clashes with the police were shown to take place at public protests in New York City, Buffalo, Philadelphia, Detroit, Minneapolis, Salt Lake City, Seattle, Portland, Louisville, Indianapolis, Los Angeles, and Oakland during these ten days. These video makers always identified the police as the aggressors, acting with impunity and malice toward the public. The police were seen as "hostile invaders in our communities" (@midwesthunny83) and expressing that to seek police help was to extend an invitation for violence (@MikiTakesPhotos).

Protesters using Twitter added that the use of tear gas was unnecessarily cruel and a "war crime" (@ewsong), claiming that the use of tear gas on crowds is a violation of the Geneva Convention (@cbundy711). Twitter users claimed that the police fully understood that rubber bullets used at protests "are life threatening, but still use them anyway" (@shivorsomething), and "shooting with rubber bullets is a P.R.-friendly way to murder black people" (@MilesBowe). Photos of officers taking aggressive positions against what appear to be peaceful protesters were commonplace in the tweets we sampled, as officers were continuously identified in tweets as being the cause of violence during nationwide protests.

At protests, the police were always seen as the aggressors who were eager to instigate violence among the protesters, who posted videos and photos showing:

Panic taking place after an officer pointed a gun at a crowd in Los Angeles.

(@timfalls)

An unarmed man on a bicycle being clubbed by several officers in New York City during a protest, where it is claimed that the police are showing "the rest of humanity the power-hungry monsters they truly are".

(@Maneuverbeard)

Retweeted video of police teargas of Seattle protesters, accused of being the aggressors in attacking a 9-year old girl.

(@frivas_917)

Uniformly, writers viewed the police violence taking place at protests as being "totally unwarranted and indefensible" (@zungumuza). One author noted these images of police violence being circulated on Twitter were "Nothing New, Just Caught on Tape" (@AF3IRMLA) while another expressed that all the circulating videos of police violence is "just the tip of the iceberg, folks" (@ajholmesmusic). #Abolish is about "drastic change from a system that targets, beats, and murders people regularly and gets away with it" (@scretladyspider).

#Abolish as Racism: The "Slave Patrol" Frame

While a large number of tweets using this hashtag specifically discuss police violence, there is also an enormous amount of overlap, which connects this violence to systemic racism, making it difficult to discuss these two sections in a separate manner. Overall, there is a strong and common link between these two beliefs, as writers often identified policing in the United States as a racist institution. Several defined American police forces as a purposely racist institution that was created specifically to oppress black people, one which has no capacity or intent to serve minority publics in a positive and supportive manner. A number of tweets within this framework identified police violence as being embedded in the origins of racial dominance and slave patrols refer to Angela Davis. People tweeted memes which quote her various writings to illustrate the inherent conflict between black lives and the US police.

The existence of American police was often said to date back to slave-era Britain, which was brought to the United States to be used on plantations as "slave patrols" – a legal authority employed to dominate blacks through intimidation and brutality against people of color. There were also writers who used #AbolishThePolice to pursue a socialist political agenda on Twitter who defined the origins of American police as an amalgamation of 1838 Boston strikebreakers and the Slave Patrol, identifying the institution as one designed to oppress people based on both race and class (@ValSorpresa).

As shown in the photo in Figure 2.1, one author posted a photo of a "Runaway Slave Patrol" badge from the 1850s and a modern-day police officer badge, noting how they have a nearly identical design, with the author adding "always remember who they are" (@Pure_Resilienc3).

In another effort to further bridge the concept of slave patrols with modern-day policing, one tweet offered a photo of the New York Police Department (NYPD) logo as seen on a squad car (replication shown in Figure 2.2) noting that the character on the left appears to be holding a whip, suggesting that the very roots of the department are embedded in the practice of slave patrolling (@imFromGhana).

FIGURE 2.1

FIGURE 2.2

Within this frame, police are viewed as the enemy of racially diverse urban communities. In more than 30 tweets, police are specifically identified to be "white supremacists" who act as "a racist institution which protect the privileged in society with violence" (@abshoots). Tweets suggest that police still continue to have an antipathy for people of color, and departments still hold cultural values that racialize crime and devalue the lives of black people, justifying acts of violence. These authors insist that these historical roots are still visible in police practices today, which is said to explain why we see racial disproportionality in arrests, convictions, and excessive use of force toward people of color. Readers are implored to resist the idea that police forces can be reformed, insisting that it was never their intention to protect black communities but rather to control minority communities to protect the interests of white Americans.

Moreover, the police were seen as unable to be reformed because, to begin with, the institution was never created to serve the interest of communities. As one Tweet states, "Reform implies an earlier time when policing embraced some sort of racial justice; if black people have never been treated fairly by police, then they cannot be reformed" (@BlkSocWithQTNA) while another writer adds "You can't reform an institution founded on, fueled and funded by racism" (@KathrynSarena). Other tweets about racism among that police included the following:

> Police are currently functioning "as it is designed" (@finchymonger) in that "It was built to protect white power and authority" (@Captain_Peanutz).

> Reform is not only impossible, it's inconceivable—it is purposely designed to harm people of color" (@snnsmith), where police are a system this is "abusing and killing black people" (@WeKeepUs).

> "#AbolishThePolice because slave catchers can't be reformed" (@eiayay), while Columbus police chief is told to "find a new job. Slave catching is over!" (@drkoach).

> Abolition is "only real solution to systemic racist, violent institution" (@DemWrite), because "As long as cops exist, they will continue to arrest and kill black people" (@heartcavemusic).

Even when a reform to weed out racism among the police was attempted among law enforcement, no effective changes are achieved. For example, one writer retweeted a story about how a series of FBI investigations into the presence of white supremacist police officers "led to no changes, no arrests, and resolved nothing" (@C_Rich75). Another author discounted FBI investigations of the police, which served largely to act as a mirage for reform but actually serve as "a shield for police aggressors" (@ConMijente).

#Abolish as Anti-Police: The "Reform Rejection" Frame

As illustrated throughout the "slave patrol" frame, tweets often claimed that police exist solely to prevent justice and equality for people of color. As a result, they use excessive violence because they were purposely designed to devalue black lives and to actively prevent justice and liberty for racial minorities. Moreover, this is a systemic process. Law enforcement is performing precisely as they were designed to do – making reform efforts pointless and destined to fail. Repeatedly found throughout the "Reform Rejection" framework are writers expressing feelings of anger and futility about police reform. Their central assumption is that police are simply beyond redemption, incapable of serving the public in a humanitarian way, and therefore should be eliminated immediately.

Writers viewed police institutions as unwilling to reform themselves and would never willingly do so while purposely doing everything in their power to avoid public accountability. There is a continual assertion that police officers (and their departments) resent and resist all calls to hold them more responsive or accountable to the public when facing accusations of misconduct. Even in cases where officers pursued reform or accountability from fellow officers and their departments, they are often pressured into resigning, a point made as proof that police cannot be reformed internally (@MichelleHux).

By and large, scathingly pessimistic opinions about effective reform were plentiful. Among the critiques about effective reform are the following viewpoints:

> #Abolish is about starting over because the system is too corrupt to be reformed through tweaks (@TravelingNun).

> As long as the police exist, they will always find a way around polices. (@Duhlency) and that Police "reforms" will be "measures they can selectively enforce" (@Tailpoof).

> You can pass all the laws you want. If there's no mechanism for forcing compliance, the cops will ignore it every time (@bmacconnell1).

> Police reform will only rearrange the racist pieces into less murderous ones (@ ElginBailey).

> "Police reform means the good guys pinky-swear to stop strangling people" (@SleepyDjango).

Tweets shared a variety of stories about large urban area police departments who have continually denied that there is any need for reform while also refusing to investigate or arrest officers accused of committing crimes. A widely circulated media text came in the form of excerpts from the NYPD commissioner from a June 9 press conference where he angrily blamed the media for vilifying their police force during the protests taking place. He is accused of being completely oblivious to the large number of videotaped cases of NYPD brutality that were circulating at a high volume on social media. The sharing of these clips is offered as a prime example of how police are unwilling to admit that the problem of police abuse even exists and are wholly unwilling to address issues of reform or accountability at all. Widely circulated stories also claimed that officers in Philadelphia, Buffalo, and Los Angeles (along with New York City) were protesting and leaving their jobs because the public has begun to demand more transparency and accountability for excess violence. Others circulated stories where officers had rallied behind fellow officers under investigation after being accused of corruption or a violent crime as evidence that police are more concerned about themselves than their public duties.

In addition to officers denying the existence of a problem with violence, criminal justice administrators and politicians were also seen as defenders of the police, acting as a structure that served to prevent reform. There were retweeted stories about district attorneys in Los Angeles who refused to prosecute cops for murder (@dijoni) and a police department that had long protected abusive cops (@RoseCoSouthWest) where people have been "Murdered by LAPD" and that "no officers are ever prosecuted" (@AF3IRMLA). There were also news stories on Twitter about how Minneapolis Police Department had consistently fought accountability and oversight measures for many years, fueling protest demands for abolition.

While there was an enormous amount of pessimism pertaining to police being capable of reforming themselves, there were also several tweets which focused upon how other institutions had failed to hold police accountable or who acted as obstacles to meaningful reforms. Police dysfunction was often portrayed as being enabled by the failures of other institutions to provide oversight, reform, and accountability. As an example, one writer claimed to support abolishing the police because there are "no effective accountability mechanisms left" (@LalehKhalili) while focusing on two specific institutional enablers: politicians and mass media.

Politicians were depicted as either unwilling or unable to bring about any effective police reforms. As a summation of these viewpoints, one writer posted a political cartoon where the GOP elephant is outraged by anyone mentioning the need to reform police while the Democrat donkey gives a long, waffling answer lacking any true convictions about change (@wrackune). In general, politicians were accused of being endlessly engaged in pursuing meaningless half-measure attempts at reform which constantly fail to effectively hold the police to any higher levels of ethical behavior or public accountability. Reform attempts were devalued as "beyond useless" (@bmacconnell1) and as "feel-good policies" (@FirestormCoop) that are introduced to the public mainly to "placate the sensibilities of white Americans" (@bmacconnell1).

As an example of the futility of reform efforts, a variety of tweets actively criticized the pragmatic, reform-based approach being championed by Democratic political leaders known as the "8 can't wait" initiative. As discussed earlier, these proposed reforms called for changes to police tactics, such as banning chokeholds, requiring all police force to be documented in writing and giving a verbal warning before using a firearm, among other things. Tweets indexed under the #Abolish hashtag openly scoffed at these ideas as "weak", "derivative", "obsolete", "tepid", "ineffectual", "lazy", and "useless". Some of those criticisms included the following comments:

> Our leaders are still pushing the exact same 'solutions' that have been getting pushed for decades (@angryblkhoemo).

> Portland politicians were mocked for approving reform over abolition, cutting only a small fraction of the force's *"huge budget"*, noting thirty years of failed *"incremental changes"* that *"did nothing to change the culture of Portland police"* (@lilithxsinclair).

Reform-oriented politicians and parties were widely ridiculed for overlooking a long history of failed reform policies and laws while continuing to offer new ones or for simply repackaging old ideas as new initiatives. Reform proposals were continuously discarded as "fake" (@danielzklein) or "flawed ideas" (@brockbooneLAW). Critics noted that many of these proposed "new" laws had already been passed, existed on paper, but are continually not enforced (such as banning chokeholds or forcing police to wear body cameras). Yet, government leaders, especially members of the Democratic Party, were "still pushing the exact same 'solutions' that have been getting pushed for decades" (@angryblkhoemo) that have "failed time and time again" (@danielzklein). Members of the Democratic Party often faced rejection from writers, viewing these politicians as not fully committed to meaningful, transformative, necessary changes. The following quote exemplifies the skepticism expressed to reform-oriented Democrats, especially at ones who refused to recognize the police as a racist institution:

> Any Democrat saying "DEFUND" the police instead of saying we need to "PUNISH" the police for killing Blacks, that person is NOT your ally.
>
> *(@cyborgK9)*

Another institution that received quite a bit of negative sentiment within this framework was the US mass media. Many authors together accuse mass media broadcasts of creating pro-police frameworks in their coverage. Television news coverages of protests were often accused of being thinly veiled public relations stunts by the police, ones enabled by television reporters, purposely made to quell protester support among the general public. Intense anger was often directed at news coverage of police being depicted as the peacemakers at protests, who were "commonly" shown to respect protesters by "taking a knee" at protests. Writers urged readers to dismiss these television news stories and images as "Copaganda" or the spreading a false narrative of police as peaceful to the public, serving to undermine the efforts of protesters. Likewise, news networks were said to be doing an extremely poor job of explaining to the public what "abolish the police" actually means in the academic literature (@rolandsmartin). Beyond the protests that were taking place, mass media creators were referred to as "scum" for having a long history of normalizing aggressive policing and glorifying officers in media content as "bad asses" when airing television shows such as *Cops* (@BlockaIsBack).

It is hard to overstate how much the failure of law enforcement to investigate and prosecute abuses of power among the police angered those who supported abolishing the police on Twitter. The abolish movement on Twitter draws much of its energy from public anger, which is an audience that widely shares the perception that police can do whatever they want and get away with it. Disgust about this condition combined with a sense that reform is an act of futility are central pillars of those who support abolishing the police.

#Abolish as Discounting the Value of Police: The "We Keep Us Safe" Frame

Tweets using the #Abolish hashtag largely had little or no confidence in reforming the police, either via internal police department actions or through external police oversight. In this discourse, some questioned if having a professionally trained police force reduced crime or effectively caught criminals at all. Within this framework, public claims about any positive contributions of law enforcement were openly questioned, and the police were depicted as a group who did not accomplish most, if any, of their stated institutional functions for the public. Accordingly, a number of writers claimed that the work currently assigned to police officers could be performed just as well, or even better, by community citizens instead.

These tweets predominantly identify the police as an ineffective institution that neither solves nor prevents crime. Instead, the police are said to exist mainly for needless surveillance of black communities. A core belief within this narrative is that communities are able to solve their problems without a police force and that the police are a cause of community problems rather than a part of their solution. Some tweeted that the police "do not reduce or prevent crime" (@EclecticRadical) and make a lot of "trash arrests", where "only 25 percent of those arrested led to convictions" (@ReenNahMean), noting that the other 75 percent of arrests are an ugly police work that was likely heavily predicated on racial profiling practices.

As an example of ineptitude, police departments were also accused of doing little to prevent violence against women and keep women safe. Police were accused of being thoroughly ineffective at preventing crimes such as rape and had commonly failed to prosecute cases of domestic violence. It was offered that "police are not needed for law and order" (@LouisaJulius) and that "police are largely unnecessary" (@authorsahunt). Readers were asked to focus on improving communities in ways that reduce crime organically without the use of law enforcement, which will eliminate any need for police surveillance and control, especially in the long run. Their central tenet is that "strong communities make police obsolete" (@GabrielMCortez) and that "We don't need police, we need to strengthen our communities and rid ourselves of the corruption" (@PoliceThePolic1).

Again, as seen within the other frames as well, there is a very high level of aggravation about the perception of racism and a rampant use of excessive force. It was offered in one tweet that 1,112 people were killed by cops in the United States during 2019, adding that "in America it is more dangerous to be policed than it is to be police" (@fxbgdsa). Many expressions of anger were voiced in regard to statistics such as this, as were palpable frustrations connecting this violence to perceptions of racism, as well as a sense of despair about achieving police reform. Some examples from our sample include:

WE DO NOT NEED TO BE POLICED (@Tinu) and BLACK FOLKS WILL DECIDE HOW BLACK FOLKS WILL FIGHT FOR OUR OWN LIVES (@DMVBlackLives).

A Minneapolis protester wants to abolish, saying "We don't need them. We don't want them. They abuse us and harass us and kill us. Now is the time" (@DanielleMuscato).

We have nothing to lose but our cops (@RedCaucus) and No more training. No more reforms. No more funding. NO MORE (@DebKilroy).

#Abolish as Defund and Redistribute: The "Opportunity Cost" Frame

Within this frame, readers were asked to defund the police to stop political leaders from "pouring billions of dollars into failed policing" (@DebKilroy). In general, these writers exhibited the least amount of hostility toward the police, and these tweets would often be indexed under both the #Abolish and #Defund hashtags simultaneously. In some cases, abolish was fully adopted as an equivalent to defunding while others connected the concept of defunding the police as a starting point for the full abolition of police in the future.

Most of these writers identified "abolish the police" as a viable long-term plan to reallocate police budgets to other community goals and resources, which were purported to eventually lead to improved levels of community health and empowerment. Here, reform "involves getting the public to see budget as value statements, get the public to IMAGINE how that money could be spent elsewhere" (@jollenelevid). Writers viewed the high levels of spending on police as an opportunity cost, where every dollar spent on policing is a dollar taken away from a much-needed community service. Stated bluntly, these redirections of funds were viewed as positive investments into "programs that don't kill black people" (@sriharshu26), an essential viewpoint commonly found under the *#AbolishThePolice* hashtag.

Overall, there was widespread agreement that police budgets were far too high and that this money did not lead to positive results for the community, where one writer stated that "There are 0 reasons to give cops more money" (@VigilantLOVEla). Tweets often documented the size of police budgets across major US cities such as New York City (@_SOLTANI), Los Angeles (@ KennethmejiaLA), and Chicago (@47Jace), pointing out that these billions of dollars spent per year could have been better spent addressing other community problems (@JanaeisAjellin). It was commonly emphasized that police forces make up a massive percentage of the city budget in most large US cities and are consistently being the largest budget line for city governments in just about every major American city (@DelvinMoody). These expenditures were said to "tower over" all other community-spending categories (@tortillabonilla), resulting in the drastic underfunding of crucial other support programs for large urban communities. Readers were urged to think about ways in which that money could be reinvested and how much better off their community would be in the long run if the police were defunded in the interest of expanding other investments that were vital for community well-being. For example, statistics provided by the ACLU were often retweeted, which identified the shortcomings readily found in community needs. Specific claims included the following (@ACLU):

- "1.7 million students are in schools with cops, but no counselors".
- "3 million students are in schools with cops, but no nurses".
- "6 million students are in schools with cops, but no school psychologists".
- "10 million students are in schools with cops, but no social workers".

While the other frameworks in this chapter often relied on vivid imagery and emotional triggers to reject the entire concept of American policing, the "Opportunity Cost" frame largely offered a more reasoned and objective approach to questioning current policing policies. More discussion of the "opportunity cost" argument for reducing the size and scope of policing will be revisited and explored in further depth in Chapter 3.

Discussion and Conclusions

While our sample located hundreds of Twitter users in support of this ambitious, controversial, and unorthodox approach to reducing crime, a number of criticisms exist. First, it has been said that there is no actual functioning model for a world without police. Places which have virtually "abolished" their police forces and prison systems still have some formal policing organization, though they are commonly smaller and are not as heavily armed (Yglesias, 2020b). In the United States, a number of rural small towns have disbanded their police departments over the years to save money. Typically, the policing duties are reliably picked up by either the county sheriff's office or a neighboring jurisdiction. However, it is doubtful if this would be feasible in large metropolitan areas, where a significantly thinner law enforcement apparatus would not be able to effectively deal with organized crime, higher rates of crime, or with violent criminals (Yglesias, 2020b).

Politically speaking, abolishing the police is also currently not a popular policy option among the American public at large. A recent public opinion poll showed that only 15 percent of Americans wanted to abolish the police (Guarino, 2020), with only slightly more support being in favor of defunding the police. While impassioned supporters are strongly in favor of abolishing the police, the movement currently faces significant political opposition. In the United States, Republicans vigorously oppose any effort to defund the police, let alone abolish it, while Democratic politicians tend to favor moderate reform proposals (Arietta-Kenna, 2020). Yet abolishing the police has garnered previously unreached levels of public attention and support during 2020, largely as a result of continued social media documentation of police violence toward people of color in the United States and outrage about a lack of police accountability.

Nevertheless, one should be careful about quickly dismissing the idea of abolishing the police out of hand. While the concept does admittedly have a fuzzy definition, public anger emanating from visceral accounts of police violence being shared on social media is palpable. It is not a stretch to think that abolishing the police will gain significantly more public support if videos of police violence continue to gain widespread public attention as they circulate online. A major shift in public opinion favoring abolition may be realized if there is a continued unwillingness of police and government to address abuse or in achieving effective reforms.

At its essence, the *#AbolishThePolice* hashtag among Twitter users served as a public forum for anger, frustration, and fear pertaining to police violence – especially toward people of color. It seems unlikely that many content creators have read much (if any) academic literature on this topic, as the online discourse was more often about emotive displays rather than reasoned debate regarding policy. While academic writers have theoretically contemplated the pros and cons of abolishing the police for years, Twitter users often support the idea largely as an anti-policy to shake up the status quo. Perceptions of the police being a detriment to their communities were the norm in our sample, with police being viewed as corrupt, violent, uncontrollable, racist, and serving little-to-no positive functions. While people can debate whether these viewpoints have merit or not, the feelings of outrage are real.

Overall, four main ideas emerged. First, *#AbolishThePolice is more about eliminating the police rather than reforming it among users of the Twitter hashtag.* Although some tweets used the hashtag to support moderate reforms for increased accountability and reduced police violence, #Abolish was more often about ending professional police forces. Additionally, while academic writers conceived of abolishing the police in a methodological fashion in terms of a policy improvement over the current form of policing, Twitter users were fueled by negative emotions and disdain for law enforcement. The overall mood among the tweets in our sample was one of anger and distrust, along with a deep-rooted pessimism in all other police reform proposals – for most hashtag contributors, abolish really does mean abolish, not reform.

Second, *those using the #AbolishThePolice hashtag commonly view the police as a racist institution that exists to purposely deprive people of color from liberty.* Consistent with some of the academic authors who support abolishing the police, forces were deemed as being too corrupt and hostile to minorities to effectively achieve meaningful positive reform. The police were continuously portrayed within the #Abolish hashtag as a self-interested institution that was full of abusive, racist, violent individuals who exhibited little concern for black lives and their communities. Tweeting within this hashtag served as an index to continually document examples of these troubling characteristics in an effort to illustrate for audiences how widespread these problems are. #Abolish is commonly used as an attempt to persuade the public to conclude that abolition is the only reasonable course of action to policing in the United States.

Third, *writers using this hashtag expressed anger and frustration toward politicians and media for their prolonged enabling of police violence against people of color.* While the academic literature was silent on this topic, the public often used Twitter to attack "beyond useless" reformist politicians and "Copaganda" news reporting. Both institutions were accused of purposely overlooking problems with policing for decades and for making insincere gestures toward meaningful reform when these problems gained widespread public attention. Readers were told to demand that politicians and their parties stop attempting unachievable reforms and embrace the abolition movement. Likewise, Twitter was used as a space to document police violence and corruption in all forms, acting as a counterweight to perceptions of mass media silence on the issue. Tweeting about the police acted as a way of framing police as the aggressors of violence against the public in ways that they believed mainstream news media would not do.

Fourth, *cities across the United States were urged to defund police and advised that they would be better served to redistribute this money into other social programs.* Police were viewed within this hashtag as an enormously expensive liability to cities, offering little return on investment for their communities. In contrast, redistributing bloated police budgets toward improving health care, education, housing, youth services, and counseling were identified as superior policy ideas that were crucial to empowering those living in urban areas. This viewpoint is largely in agreement with academic writers who also favored abolishing the police, who also think of defunding the police in terms of long-term community improvement and reduced crime. Readers were rhetorically implored to think about what was possible for their communities, and how an end to the cycle of poverty and oppression could be realized if police budget money were redirected. In sum, tweets under the #Abolish hashtag claimed that continuing to spend so much money on police led only to more of the same – more oppression, more violence, mass incarceration, and prolonged inequality – for people of color.

Notes

1 Police perceive being "at war" with the public they are supposed to be serving. It is the common mindset of police to believe all members of the community are suspicious and potentially dangerous to them.
2 UCLA director of public policy.
3 A political science professor at Syracuse University.
4 A political scientist.
5 Christy Lopez, law professor at Georgetown University.
6 Christy Lopez, law professor at Georgetown University.

References

Arietta-Kenna, R. (2020, June 12). The deep roots – and new offshoots – of 'abolish the police. *Politico*. www. politico.com/news/magazine/2020/06/12/abolish-defund-police-explainer-316185

Bergman, M. (2018). Police shootings and race in the United States: Why the perpetrator predation perspective is essential to I-O psychology's role in ending this crisis. *Industrial and Organizational Psychology, 119*(1), 1–6.

Bleich, S. N., Findling, M. G., Casey, L. S., Blendon, R. J., Benson, J. M., SteelFisher, G. K., Sayde, J. M., & Miller, C. (2019). Discrimination in the United States: Experiences of Black Americans. *Special Issue: Experiences of Discrimination in America: Race, Ethnicity, Gender, and Sexuality, 54*(S2), 1399–1408.

Bondurant, S. R., Lindo, J. M., & Swensen, I. D. (2018). Substance abuse treatment centers and local crime. *Journal of Urban Economics, 104*, 124–133.

Boyum, D. A., Caulkins, J. P., & Kleiman, M. A. R. (2011). Drugs, crime, and public policy. In J. Q. Wilson & J. Petersilia (Eds.), *Crime and public policy* (pp. 368–410). Oxford University Press.

Briond, J. (2020, June 6). Understanding the role of police towards abolitionism: On black death as an American necessary, abolition, non-violence, and whiteness. *Hampton Institute*. www.hamptonthink.org/read/understanding-the-role-of-police-towards-abolitionism-on-black-death-as-an-american-necessity-abolition-non-violence-and-whiteness

Carhado, D, W. (2017). From stopping black people to killing black people: The Fourth Amendment pathways to police violence. *California Law Review, 105*(125), 125 161.

Chandler, R. K., Fletcher, B. W., & Volkow, N. D. (2009). Treating drug abuse and addition in the criminal justice system. *JAMA, 301*(2), 183–190.

Correia, D., & Wall, T. (2017). *Police: A field guide*. Verso Books.

Cuellar, A. E., McReynolds, L. S., & Wasserman, G. A. (2006). A cure for crime: Can mental health treatment diversion reduce crime among youth? *Journal of Policy Analysis Management: [The Journal of the Association for Public Policy Analysis and Management], 25*(1), 197–214.

DeGue, S., Fowler, K., & Calkins, C. (2016). Deaths due to use of lethal force by law enforcement: Findings from the national violence death reporting system, 17 U.S. states, 2009–2012. *American Journal of Preventive Medicine, 51*(5 Suppl. 3), S173–S187.

Frank, R. G., & McGuire, T. G. (2011). Mental health treatment and criminal justice outcomes. In P. J. Cook, J. Ludwig, & J. McCrary (Eds.), *Controlling crime: Strategies and tradeoffs* (pp. 167–207). University of Chicago Press.

Gaston, S. (2019). Enforcing race: A neighborhood-level explanation of black-white differences in drug arrests. *Crime & Delinquency, 65*(4), 499–526.

Guarino, B. (2020, July 22). Few Americans want to abolish police, Gallup survey finds. *Washington Press*. www.washingtonpost.com/nation/2020/07/22/abolish-police-gallup-poll/

Illing, S. (2020, June 12). The 'abolish the police' movement, explained by 7 scholars and activists. *Vox Magazine*. www.vox.com/policy-and-politics/2020/6/12/21283813/george-floyd-blm-abolish-the-police-8cantwait-minneapolis

Jones-Brown, D., & King-Toler, E. (2011). The significance of race in contemporary urban policing policy. In K. Ismaili (Ed.), *U.S. criminal justice policy: A contemporary reader* (pp. 21–48). Jones & Bartlett Learning.

Kappeler, V. E., & Gaines, L. K. (2012). *Community policing: A contemporary perspective* (6th ed.). Elsevier Publishing.

Koch, D. W., Lee, J., & Lee, K. (2016). Coloring the war on drugs: Arrest disparities in black, brown, and white. *Race and Social Problems, 8*, 313–325.

Langergan, K. (2020, June 12). The city that really did abolish the police. *Politico*. www.politico.com/news/magazine/2020/06/12/camden-policing-reforms-313750

Liebertz, S., & Bunch, J. (2018). Examining the externalities of welfare reform: TANF and crime. *Justice Quarterly, 35*(3), 477–504.

Lochner, L. (2020). Chapter 9 – Education and crime. In S. Bradley & C. Green (Eds.), *The economics of education: A comprehensive overview* (2nd ed., pp. 109–117). Academic Press.

McDowell, M. G., & Fernandez, L. A. (2018). 'Disband, disempower, and disarm': Amplifying the theory and practice of police abolition. *Critical Criminology, 269*, 373–391.

Palmer, C., Phillips, D. C., & Sullivan, J. X. (2019). Does emergency financial assistance reduce crime? *Journal of Public Economics, 169*, 34–51.

Perry, T. (2020, June 10). America's 'most dangerous city' defunded its police department 7 years ago. It's been a stunning success. *Upworthy*. www.upworthy.com/americas-most-dangerous-city-defunded-its-police-department-7-years-ago-it-was-a-stunning-success

Pullmann, M. D. (2011). Effects of out-of-home mental health treatment on probability of criminal charge during the transition to adulthood. *American Journal of Orthopsychiatry, 81*(3), 410–419.

Purnell, D. (2017, August 23). What does police abolition mean? *Boston Review Online*. https://bostonreview.net/law-justice/derecka-purnell-what-does-police-abolition-mean

Reborido, S. (2013). A New York police department care is seen in Manhattan, New York, Sept. 16, 2013. [Photograph]. *abc News*. https://abcnews.go.com/US/york-city-police-officer-indicted-tampering-crime-scene/story?id=61871269

Rudolph, M., & Starke, P. (2020). How does the welfare state reduce crime? The effect of program characteristics and decommodification across 18 OECD-countries. *Journal of Criminal Justice, 68*(Issue C), 1–12.

Spruill, L. H. (2016). Slave patrols, "packs of negro dogs" and policing black communities. *Phylon, 53*(1), 42–66.

Van Der Werff, E. (2020, June 8). The narrative power of 'abolish the police'. *Vox Magazine*. www.vox.com/culture/2020/6/8/21281069/abolish-the-police-black-lives-matter-george-floyd-protests-minneapolis-new-york

Vitale, A. S. (2017). *The end of policing*. Verso Publishing.

Vitale, A. S., & Casleton, S. (2020, July 1). The problem isn't just police – it's politics. *Boston Review Online*. https://bostonreview.net/race-politics-law-justice/alex-vitale-scott-casleton-problem-isnt-just-police%E2%80%94its-politics

Yglesias, M. (2020a, June 5). 8 can't wait, explained. *Vox Magazine*. www.vox.com/2020/6/5/21280402/8-cant-wait-explained-policing-reforms

Yglesias, M. (2020b, June 2018). The end of policing left me convinced we still need policing. *Vox Magazine*. www.vox.com/2020/6/18/21293784/alex-vitale-end-of-policing-review

3

DEFUND THE POLICE ON TWITTER

Introduction

Due to a series of tragic and high-profile cases regarding the deaths of unarmed black Americans at the hands of police over the years, especially with the more recent examples of 2020, protesting has increased, and the calls to defund the police have become prominent. Protesting to demonstrate this demand has led to violence and an increased distrust and hatred of police. Not only has such protesting taken to the streets, but social justice seekers using social media, especially Twitter, have played a prominent role in how the nation responds to public concerns about policing in the United States, leading some to call for "defunding" the police. While the calls to defund the police during 2020 progressed, societal perceptions of what this phrase really meant were highly mixed. The public has interpreted the call to defund the police in a variety of ways, with some of these definitions in clear contrast with one another, creating unclear discourse about a topic due to definitions that are not universally shared among all discussants. In this chapter, we identify several ways in which *#DefundThePolice* was constructed by Twitter users, hoping to shed light on the variations in use.

Background Review

Throughout the history of the United States, especially within the last few decades, calls for racial equality via protests against the police have increased. Michael Brown, Eric Gardner, and Tamir Rice – names that are widely known throughout the country as examples of perceived unwarranted police violence that resulted in countrywide protests, beginning with the Ferguson Protests in 2014. During 2020, many white Americans once again became highly salient of racial inequality in American policing due to media content. Through high-profile stories distributed throughout a variety of mass and social mediums, the public was vicariously exposed to news stories of police violence and abuse. One of these cases involved the death of George Floyd at the hands of four Minneapolis police officers, with another being the death of Breonna Taylor in Louisville, Kentucky during a controversial police raid of her apartment. These news reports and images troubled many Americans. Many of these viewers were awakened to the existence of vast racial inequalities that are entrenched in the policing system, causing some to see American policing through a new

DOI: 10.4324/9781003224440-3

lens (Onwauchi-Willig, 2021; Cobbina-Dungy et al., 2022). A large number of Americans were so outraged by these various reports of police violence to engage in nationwide public protests during the summer of 2020.

Many of the protests were organized by Black Lives Matter (BLM), who openly welcomed protesters from across a variety of different race, social class, and age groups to engage in protesting against systemic racism (Cobbina-Dungy et al., 2022). During protests, demands were often made to "defund the police", calls which were echoed throughout the media landscape in response to the killings of unarmed black civilians by the police, leading to increased public discourse about the power and authority of police agencies (Cobbina-Dungy et al., 2022). Defund the police proved to be a strategic frame that resonated well with protesters, largely speaking, as they sought to reimagine policing and push for change.

Nevertheless, after several weeks of demonstrations and discourse about the concept, important gaps still remained regarding Americans' understanding of what this slogan implies when it comes to police reforms. While most Americans believed that defunding involved changing the way police departments operate on a daily basis (Murray, 2022), opinion polls were unable to identify deeper meaning people attached to these terms, nor were they able to precisely specify how policing should be practiced differently. In general, the public held inconsistent understanding, perceptions, or beliefs about the meaning of the slogan (Cobbina-Dungy et al., 2022).

Of course, this is not a surprising finding. Being a relatively new term that reflects a topic which most people do not have any expertise or direct experience with, respondents are being asked about issues to which they have given little thought, resulting in uninformed views (Dionne & Mann, 2003; Cobbina-Dungy et al., 2022). Additionally, the media ecosystem of the United States bombarded audiences with divergent claims about what defunding the police really looks like, or how it should be implemented, and what kinds of changes we should expect to see.

#DefundThePolice – Reviewing the Origin of Its Meaning

The argument over the true intention and meaning behind *#DefundThePolice* is widespread and extremely controversial. Many believe this means to completely demolish and get rid of law enforcement (e.g., Capitol Hill Autonomous Zone (CHAZ) in Seattle, Washington, and the Minneapolis City Council voting to disband the Minneapolis Police Department) while others believe it means to define the duties of law enforcement and aid other community programs. However, looking at the original meaning behind *#DefundThePolice*, as well as the meaning the Black Lives Matter (BLM) group supports, is key to understanding just how societal perceptions differ when it comes to understanding the intent behind the hashtag.

#DefundThePolice was created as a way to bring about attention to the fact that governments were slashing budgets while the budget provided to law enforcement simultaneously continued to increase. The War on Crime in the 1960s, the "Get Tough on Crime" approach of the 1990s, and police unions supporting political candidates and campaigns, has given the view that police budgets are untouchable (Jacobs & Helm, 1997; Caldeira & Cowart, 1980). As a result, budgets pertaining to education, substance abuse services and mental health services, homelessness, and many others have been cut, as demonstrated in the graphs shown in Figures 3.1 and 3.2.

With funding for other community resources decreasing, law enforcement officers were tasked with handling those underfunded services, which greatly redefines and differs from their original role of law and order enforcement. Society has asked law enforcement to shift from an approach of strictly enforcing law and order, to a community-based, problem-oriented approach (Cortright

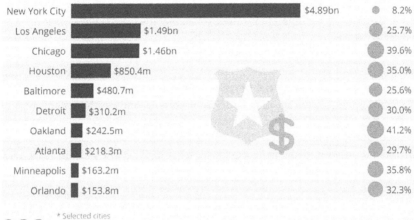

FIGURE 3.1

FIGURE 3.2

et al., 2020; Torres et al., 2018; Normore et al., 2016; Reiss Jr., 1992). This new approach expects law enforcement to not only handle but also fix a variety of social issues that they have not been properly trained to deal with. Even with research demonstrating that specialists are needed to more adequately respond to such cases (Hipple, 2017; Steadman et al., 2000; Lamb et al., 1995), and police officers reporting cases have better outcomes and are handled more successfully when they have the assistance of specialists of mobile crisis units (Borum et al., 1998), the blunt of the responsibility continues to fall directly on law enforcements' shoulders.

David Brown, a former Dallas, Texas chief of police, stated in a 2016 interview that society was asking police to do too much, by putting "every societal failure . . . off for the cops to solve . . . Policing was never meant to solve all those problems" (Bazaldua, 2016, para. 3). As a result, *#DefundThePolice* was created to bring about awareness to this overuse of law enforcement for roles they are not meant to hold while we underuse resources that we are asking law enforcement to do, simply because of a lack of funding. Thus, the overarching goal of *#DefundThePolice* is to reform the criminal justice system.

Aside from raising awareness of police department budgets, the meaning behind *#DefundThePolice* is not to get rid of police altogether, but instead to reduce their budgets for the purpose of redistributing those funds to other social programs. This money could be reallocated to areas that are often neglected, such as "education, public health, housing, and youth services" (Arnold, 2020, para. 4). In doing so, it is believed that crime rates will decrease (Arnold, 2020). As an illustrative example, if more money is put into education, especially within the inner cities where such funding is drastically lacking, more students would graduate from high school and thus have an increased chance of obtaining a legitimate job. Similarly, if more money is put into public health, mental health and substance abuse issues would be better handled and treated, and community health and prosperity would increase while crime decreases as a result. In support of this concept, all of these programs have been found to decrease the likelihood of individuals engaging in crime. For example, the Black Lives Matter movement used Twitter to post an image which called for the demilitarization of public safety, defunding of the police, and investment in communities (@BLM).

According to many of those within the Black Lives Matter movement, *#DefundThePolice* is a call to end "the systematic racism that allows this culture of corruption to go unchecked and [Black] lives to be taken" (Black Lives Matter, 2020, para. 8). Alicia Garza, a co-founder of BLM, stated the "growing calls to 'defund the police' are not about eliminating police departments, but about reallocating funds toward 'the resources that our communities need'" (Perano, 2020, para. 1). This means that they do not want to get rid of law enforcement, but they want to transform the "racist system that breeds corruption" and make changes so that law enforcement will be held "accountable for the violence they inflict, and create a system ensuring equality for Blacks" (BLM, 2020, para. 11). They call for a national defunding of police and investing such money in the communities and resources "to ensure Black people not only survive, but thrive" (BLM, 2020, para. 9). This means putting less money toward law enforcement and reinvesting that money back into the community.

Frameworks of "#DefundThePolice" Found on Twitter

After careful analysis of the *#DefundThePolice* tweet sample, we have identified four unique frameworks. We have given these frames the following titles, with a brief summary of common themes and assumptions most often found within these frames in bullet-points format:

1. "Nothing but Trouble"

- The public displays anger toward the police.
- Police are accused of being racist.
- Police are accused of being violent, even act as terrorists.
- Police are said to be above the law.

2. "Reform and Reallocate"

- A more "pro-police" tone, which purports a more community policing approach which does not require expensive militaristic weapons, justifying budget cuts.

- Budget cuts are done without hostility toward police, recognize their work as necessary and difficult, but still in need of significant changes/reforms.
- Writers encourage public to be imaginative in thinking about new policies and approaches, to explore the opportunity costs of taxpayer money, particularly in thinking about how funds could be moved to community investments and other preventive measures to reduce crime rates in the long term.

3. "Phase Out and Restart"

- Defunding police is viewed as "a first step" in the ultimate goal of abolishing police departments; writers are highly critical of police and display dissatisfaction for the institution.
- Anti-police writers suggest defunding as a politically acceptable half-measure toward abolishing the police; if we cannot immediately eliminate the police, then "fewer police is better" in the short run as the community should pursue full abolishment as a long-term policy objective.
- Police viewed as a "poor investment" of taxpayer money, often refers to statistics that show continued high crime rates, low arrest rates, small percentage of successful prosecutions, low rates of crime prevention, and so on despite high amounts of budget expense per year.

4. "World Without Police"

- Writers use defund the police to essentially call for an end to policing.
- Expressing a widespread belief that the police are not necessary or beneficial for the community and that the work of dealing with crime/deviance can be done by nonprofessional citizens.
- Tweets were used to illustrate life without police, citing examples such as Minneapolis, Seattle, and Camden, New Jersey as places where the police were replaced.

The remainder of this chapter will provide the readers with a detailed examination of how these frameworks were constructed, using posted photos and direct quotes to illustrate central claims, as well as exploring assumptions which were made by these authors.

The "Nothing but Trouble" Frame

As demonstrated later, key themes in terms of perceptions of law enforcement, demonstrated via the content analysis of the tweets containing the hashtag *#DefundThePolice*, show a range of societal perceptions of law enforcement. Such themes range from complete support of law enforcement to a call to completely get rid of law enforcement.

Anger Toward the Police

Anger toward the police can be demonstrated via the 2020 protests, in which police precincts have been burned to the ground, and police statues and monuments have been vandalized and destroyed by protestors. @bellykachman demonstrated anger toward police due to her own past experiences with them:

> Law & Order SVU is a rape girl's favorite bedtime fairy tale yes but did I go to the police when I was NO do I know any survivors who have been helped by the police NO do I know survivors who have been raped by the police YES do I trust the police NO FUCKING NO #DefundThePolice.

Others demonstrated visceral and dehumanizing displays of anger without providing specific reason for why they felt this way, such as a photo that was both drawn and tweeted by @moshminski. The photo states "DRAIN THE PIGS FEED THE REST" encircling three bloody decapitated pig heads with money falling from their necks.

A third group of individuals demonstrated anger toward police as resulting from past events law enforcement have participated in, such as that of the Tamir Rice shooting and incidents that occurred during the 2020 protests.

> [W]hat fucks me up to this very minute is that Tamir Rice's murderer didn't even try NOT to use deadly force. Your reflex is to pull up and shoot? Tamir being a 12 yr old kid didn't even register to him. A CHILD! #DefundThePolice #AbolishThePolice.
>
> *(@DwayneDuggerII)*

> All 57 of the police officers resigned in protest. Sounds good right? WRONG! They resigned in support of the two officers who were suspended for pushing an elderly man. It's not just a couple bad apples. It's so very clearly not. #DefundThePolice.
>
> *(@Slicebananas)*

In response to a tweet about former Buffalo police officer Cariol Horne, which @WillMcAvoy-ACN stated would "be tough to read at times, and . . . will feature several 'triggers'", @tomperriello stated: "Not just a few bad apples, but the whole system. Also, can we stop using 'bad apples' as a placeholder for evil torturers and murderers hiding behind the badge? #DefundThePolice". Within this tweet, @tomperriello stated that police as a collective whole, and not just individual officers, were violent, suggesting violence committed by law enforcement was more of a systemwide issue than just a case of a "few bad apples".

Even when law enforcement demonstrated kneeling in solidarity, they were still looked at as being in the wrong, with them kneeling being seen as nothing more than a photo op. @Bluvband, in sharing a news video showing police across the country kneeling in solidarity, stated: "Do not buy into this! This is just propaganda. These same cops also beat the shit out of innocent people when the curfews kicked in, so don't try to distract us with your lies". @VarishaMK supported this notion saying that police kneeling in support means nothing and is pointless if they do not believe in making a change: "Kneeling with protestors means nothing if you don't believe police violence is a systemic American problem. Kneeling with protestors means nothing if you don't take de-escalation seriously. #DefundThePoice". This, along with the photo shared by @LibQn32, suggests that even when police officers are attempting to demonstrate their support for the Black Lives Matter movement, or that they themselves are of a minority race, they are still bad individuals because of their chosen profession. Characteristically, when individuals demonstrated anger toward law enforcement, such anger tends to be accompanied with references to law enforcers as violent or racist, as demonstrated in a photo tweeted by @LibQn32. The photo depicts a female minority officer in uniform, with the words "When you say FTP [fuck the police], you're saying that to me too". @LibQn32 tweeted the photo stating "Yep, 100 Fuck her too! #DefundThePolice", demonstrating a dislike of all police officers and not just a select group.

A key slogan that further establishes the anger and hatred toward law enforcement is that of *#ACAB*, an acronym for "all cops are bastards". As demonstrated in the following tweets, which contain both the *#ACAB* hashtag and the *#DefundThePolice* hashtag, anger toward law enforcement is evident. Tweets using this hashtag added the following:

Cops are literally the most emotionally unstable cowards. They are scared of unarmed people, easily upset by protestors WORDS and get trigger happy at the sight of ANYONE, including media. THIS ISNT HALO!".

(@joidm210)

This is EXACTLY why using tear gas during a pandemic is basically the same as using a biological weapon. Covid19 is a respiratory illness that is only exacerbated and easily spread by the effects of the tear gas! Now someone is DEAD because of it!

(@PasswordSuck2)

Although the tweets containing *#ACAB* in combination with *#DefundThePolice* tended to demonstrate more outright and clear anger toward law enforcement, anger toward law enforcement is evident in tweets containing just *#DefundThePolice*.

Police Are Racist

Describing law enforcement as a racist system was a prominent theme among the sample. As demonstrated by the following tweets, not only was the system deemed racist, but specified departments and law enforcement officers themselves were deemed racist as well.

No one needs a probe to find out if a police department is racist. POLICING IS RACIST. Its roots, its practice, its purpose are all irrefutably anti-Black. The only reform is #DefundPolice! That's it! Say it with me! #BlackLivesMatter #JusticeForGeorgeFloyd #DefundThePolice.

(@radfagg)

The Communist Party stands in solidarity with the ongoing rebellion against racist murders by police in both Canada and the US. #DefundThePolice & end the repression!

(@compartycanada)

The working class in Central Texas knows what side we're on. We're fighting to defund the police to stop racist police violence. Join us for our discussion Friday with Alex Vitale! Let's #DefundThePolice.

(@austin_DSA)

In order to defund hatred & racism in our messed up criminal justice system, elected officials need to show up and commit to #DefundThePolice in memory of #GeorgeFloyd #BreonnaTaylor #AhmaudAubrey & countless others.

(@sara_arub)

After countless hours of organizing, we are glad the city has chosen to finally disband the Gun Violence Reduction Team, Portland's racist gang policing unit. However, this is only a start.

(@carenotcops)

The @LAPDHQ is racist, supremacist, and murderous. Angelenos want to #DfundThePolice and invest in #CareNotCops. @CD6Nury.

(@iamKITTENS)

Due to the unwarranted killing of black people, as well as the perceived history of policing, it is believed that not only are law enforcement officers themselves racist, but departments as a whole are racist. This is in part due to the perceived history of policing, which has created the belief that policing itself is rooted in racist beginnings and a racist US history.

Police Are Violent

As can be seen in several of the tweets demonstrating anger toward law enforcement, there is evidence of viewing police as being violent. Additionally, several tweets within the sample demonstrated the belief in police being outright violent. @ArchCityDefense referred to the police as being extremely violent, stating: "In FY19, want to know how much of your tax dollars #STLCity/@LydaKrewson invested in one of the most brutal, lethal police departments in the entire county?" Similarly, @NotAnarchyball stated how tax money supports a brutality machine. @BLMChi called for "an end to the system of state sanctioned violence through policing & white supremacist vigilantes". Others provided examples of law enforcement violence:

> That's Bullshit. I was at a protest that was peaceful. People were standing in the streets, but people were not inciting things. The police were. They were pepper spraying peaceful protestors & tackling small women who were just standing in the street.
>
> *(@PepperOceanna)*

> Only #DefundThePolice can stop this. (@ChuckModi1) ◊ Oklahoma cop says police are shooting Black Americans "less than we probably ought to be".
>
> *(@RawStory)*

> Today 4 more videos of Black and Brown men being killed by the police have just been released because of journalists suing, lawyers sharing and pressure from community groups.
>
> *(@rosaclemente)*

In terms of referring to the police as violent, instead of outright calling them violent, law enforcement officers were referred to as terrorists instead.

> The police are the ones rioting! They are terrorist in tax funded uniforms.
>
> *(@themariefonseca)*

> The NYPD are biological + viral terrorists for not wearing face masks and knowingly continuing the spread of COVID-19. They aren't thugs or animals; they are a domestic terrorist organization and do not care about their own health or the health of the city. #DefundThePolice.
>
> *(@aquariaofficial)*

> Police are TRAINED to kill and carry out acts of terror on Black communities to ensure that the racial caste system never dies. We need to #DefundThePolice.
>
> *(@sunrisemvmt)*

Proud Boys are just another arm of the KKK and these cops showing favorites show why we need to disarm, defund and demilitarize the police!

(@mikesmyman1)

With the examples of police violence provided in the tweets, as well as outright calling law enforcement a violent system, there was a shared belief that officers themselves could be different. Previously tweets called out law enforcement for kneeling – calling it nothing more than a photo op and pointless. However, one tweet believed that if police did stand against their fellow officers, then society would stop viewing all police officers as bad cops.

Until they stand up against their fellow officers all police will be considered bad cops who conduct.

(@quintonmassimo)

Such a tweet demonstrates the possibility that segments of society who believe all police officers are bad and violent could change their perceptions of such officers, as long as those officers are willing to stand up against the "bad apples" and make a stand to stop police brutality.

Police Are Above the Law

While not highly demonstrated in the tweets, there is a societal perception that law enforcement officers are above the law. This means that they can do whatever they want without fear of legal consequences due to being in law enforcement. Essentially, it is believed since they are in law enforcement, they can get away with anything and everything, including illegal actions, because other law enforcement officers will not arrest them due to the whole "thin blue line" aspect. The "thin blue line" will be discussed in a later chapter.

@SieberforORD1 accused law enforcement of murdering innocent individuals due to the reward of getting a paid vacation during the investigation into the incident. In response to the Portland Mayor directing the Portland Police Chief to not use teargas "UNLESS there is a 'serious and immediate threat to life safety, and there is no other viable alternative for dispersal'", @PortlandDSA demonstrated how law enforcement will always do what they want because of the power they have:

This is typical of most liberal attempts at police reform. No matter how their training manual or Mayor might ask them to behave they will always choose to act as violently as they please because they have the power to do so. We need to #DefundThePolice and take away this power.

With the defund movement aiming to take away police power, @AdrienneLaw explained what she believed law enforcement would do to maintain such power:

With the movement to #DefundThePolice, be prepared for law enforcement to do everything in their power to try to justify their jobs – e.g., exploiting math, increased unnecessary arrests, enhanced overcharging, planting more evidence, etc.

Such tweets suggest that police officers can get away with whatever they want because of their occupation and that they will do whatever is necessary to maintain such power.

The "Reform and Reallocate" Frame

Such tweets demonstrate the crucial need to reallocate funds to the appropriate services, which the government defunded and left to the responsibility of law enforcement. Instead of allowing trained professionals to handle mental health, addiction, homelessness, and other prevalent, specialized issues, politicians decided the burden of fixing these issues resided with law enforcement; thus they placed such a heavy burden on the shoulders of an agency who is unqualified to handle such issues. Thus, to allow police to better serve their community, community services need to be refunded by allocating the funding given to law enforcement so they could attempt to address these issues, back to the programs where individuals were trained to adequately handle such issues. Doing so would not only effectively address many of the societal problems we have but would also take the burden off of law enforcement and allow them to better assist the community in the role they were meant to have.

Figure 3.3, which is a rendering of the graphic tweeted by @Craven7Jessica, was made to clarify to readers *an attempt to form a more clear definition* of what #DefundThePolice is referring to.

#DefundThePolice means
- Police will be funded
- Police will not be overfunded
- Redistribute the city budget
- Everyone gets a fair share

#DefundThePolice because
- Police should focus on crimes and criminals
- Police are not mental health counselors
- Police are not social workers
- Police are not medical professionals
- Police are not education specialists
- Police should not be responsible for everything

#DefundThePolice emphasizes
- Reassessing our values
- Investing in our communities
- Investing in our people
- Funding our schools
- Funding our hospitals
- Funding our services
- Funding our infrastructure

Understand that presenting "defund the police" as the same as "eliminating al funding for police" is intentionally misleading and manipulative.

FIGURE 3.3

Several of the tweets, while not only demonstrating what *#DefundThePolice* means, also explained more specifically how to go about doing so.

What does it mean when people say #DefundThePolice? It means reducing the scale, scope & power of police, by reallocating city budget $$ from policing to human-centered services.

(@WomanProjectHQ)

What a sample of PART of #DefundThePolice could look like. Portugal switched drug abuse from a criminal issue to a health care issue. Instead of cops and jail, drug users got doctors and rehab. Portugal's drug deaths and related issues PLUMMETED. Ending the war on drugs.

(@SjwSpiderman)

As a former local elected official who has led a couple of movement . . . I am in support of the call to #DefundThePolice. @ZyahnaB can tell you . . . I was completed against their, & thought it was a horrible idea . . . until being educated on it. To be honest, it makes a lot of sense. I have spoken to and/or heard thousands of police officers say "We are not equipped to solve every issue that we are called for. I am not a psychologist, I am not a social worker, people don't know how hard his job is". If that is true, why not provide resources to others? Local governments 4 example, operate w/ budgets that are contingent on a variety of issues. You would be hard pressed to find a budget that does not have the largest portion of its resources going to law enforcement. That HAS to change in order for our communities to change. So when people say #DefundThePolice, extrapolating "some" of the resources that they (police) currently receive, and moving them to social workers, to education, after school programs, mental health workers, etc. to some of the things that current police can't address, is key. When you look at middle class/affluent communities, you see resources, you see access, you see a lower police presence. Often, when you see low income communities, you have little to no resources, access, & high presence of police. THIS has to change&Budgets need 2be redirected. Lastly, when we talk about #DefundThePolice, we have to dare ourselves to think differently. We need Public Safety in all communities, which is different from law enforcement. The 2 terms are not interchangeable. De-Funding does not mean dismantling.

(@DrWesBellamy)

While also defining the movement, two tweets specifically mentioned how funding other programs was necessary, as the police were currently required to engage in tasks that they were not meant to or trained to do, causing police to take on too much.

So lets understand what Defund Police means. It actually HELPS cops, not harm them. Because it relieves them of duties they attend to now that are not under their umbrella and which are best served by professionals like psychologists and mental health experts. #DefundThePolice.

(@MrDash109)

We are asking the police to do too much. We've defunded vital departments (mental health, drug addiction, community services) & left it to police. We desperately need to #DefundThePolice & appropriately allocate those resources not just for the benefit of communities, but police.

(@AnnaAkana)

The "reform and reallocate" frame would often make some reference to the *#8Can'tWait campaign*, a popular campaign that has commonly accompanied *#DefundThePolice* and fits with the true meaning of the hashtag is *#8CantWait*, created by the Zero Campaign in June 2020, in response to the George Floyd incident. The goal of the *#8CantWait* campaign is to reform the police by making specific and concrete immediate changes to police departments. In total, there are eight policies that *#8CantWait* encourages cities to adopt, which included the following reforms (Campaign Zero, 2020):

- Ban chokeholds and strangleholds
- Require de-escalation techniques
- Require a warning before shooting
- Exhaust all other alternatives before shooting
- Emphasize a duty for other officers to intervene
- Ban shooting at moving vehicles
- Establish a use of force continuum
- Require all uses of force to be reported

While calling to defund the police, people have suggested that these eight changes be immediately adopted by all police departments, stating that such adoption cannot wait, otherwise there would be more black lives that will be harmed during the wait.

Campaign Zero (2020), upon examining rates of police violence in cities that had use of force restrictions compared to cities that did not have such restrictions, found the suggested restrictions decrease police violence by 72 percent. Fyfe (1979) examined the effectiveness of a restrictive use of force policy, adopted by the NYPD, which banned shooting at people in moving vehicles and required officers to use lesser alternatives when possible instead of automatically relying on deadly force. It was found that using just two of the eight *#8CantWait* suggested policies significantly decreased civilian injuries and killings and also police injury and killings. Philadelphia, in 1980, adopted a restrictive use of force policy, which lead to a 67 percent decrease in fatal shootings within the first year of adoption, even after police shootings had been steadily decreasing at an average of 20 percent per year from 1974 until this time (White, 2000). In addition, after the *Tennessee v. Garner* decision in 1985, in which the United States Supreme Court adopted a more restrictive use of force policy by ruling that laws which authorized "police use of deadly force to apprehend fleeing, unarmed, non-violent felony suspects" violated the Fourth Amendment (Tennenbaum, 1994, p. 241), police killings country-wide dropped by 16 percent. Supporters of this movement posted the following under the *#DefundThePolice* hashtag:

> If elected, I will require ALL SC law enforcement agencies to adopt the #8cantwait policies immediately. Required de-escalation & a uniform use of force continuum would have saved Jamal's life. A duty to intervene would have required others to stop what was happening.
>
> *(@Gary4GovSC)*

> I'm joining #8CantWait to urge local mayors to enact policies that have the power to reduce police killings that results in death in our major cities. I urge you to join me. We simply can't wait – too much is at stake. Learn more: 8cantwait.org.
>
> *(@rfhbill)*

However, in contrast to the limited support of the *#8CantWait* campaign, a large majority of individuals on Twitter vocalized criticisms with the campaign. One individual in particular called the campaign's statistical practices into question. @RolandWNoBrakes said, "I feel like the issues with social media is it catapults people without in-depth knowledge or professional background into these positions they're not ready for. Someone without any statistical training or stats work experience basically did the #8cantwait stats" while @SFath called the methodology into question –

"it comes from a study for which the methodology seems to be flawed". Others believe that the campaign fails to adequately address the racial issue within policing and quite frankly is just a weak liberal attempt to appease society:

> #REJECT8CantWait. 8CantWait proposal is just an attempt to make everyone feel like they've done something and fool people into thinking the problem is solved. It changes nothing. We need to #DefundThePolice.
>
> *(@JRaphling)*

> Join our statement, #8CantWait is a toothless set of demands that doesn't target fundamental ways & racist underpinnings that govern policing. It serves as a valve to release pressure & distracts from the movement to #Defundthepolice & end the violence and killings of Black ppl.
>
> *(LACANetwork)*

> #8cantwait is an accomplice to state violence. #REJECT8cantwait.
>
> *(@LexStepp)*

> [C]ities are scrambling to implement #8cantwait before they're forced to dismantle their police depts. 8cantwait might be the single most detrimental thing for the movement that isn't an actual police dept. don't compromise on justice don't compromise on justice.
>
> *(@casseroleboy)*

> Tbh I'm uncertain about the #8CantWait proposition – technically yes, this would implement some systemic change. But last I checked cops don't give a single f*ck about following rules. That's literally why this movement started.
>
> *(@skincarebyhyram)*

Others demonstrated how departments who have had such policy recommendations implemented, still have issues.

> Great example here of why reforming police policies is not enough to keep us safe. Lawrence PD adhere to all 8 proposed #8cantwait solutions, yet the policies did not prevent an unarmed Black man from being shot in the back during a traffic stop in 2018.
>
> *(@Dev_Der)*

> The MPD implemented all the reforms in the 8cantwait campaign and Derek Chauvin, a cop with 17 misconduct complaints overlooked, still killed George Floyd. Reform killed George Floyd, and all other names we are currently chanting in the streets. Abolish the fucking police.
>
> *(@Jahdi_)*

> #PasadenaPolice shot a man in his back and killed him, maced witnesses, and are pressing charges on a protestor. PPD has #8cantwait in place.
>
> *(@LexStepp)*

Many good proposals to improve policing policies have been offered over the past week that should be enacted. But material change is harder than just changing laws or words in the employee handbook. "Culture eats strategy for breakfast", is true in most orgs, including PDs.

The #8cantwait campaign claims that enacting the slate of reforms "can decrease police violence by 72% (versus having none of these policies)". I'm skeptical it's this easy. Enacting policies without culture change is helpful but limited. After Laquan McDonald shooting, the DOJ sent a team in to investigate the Chicago PD. A member of that team later told me Chicago had better policies than his last department. The problem wasn't policies; it was that officers weren't following the policies on the streets. NYPD banned choke holds in 1994; Eric Garner died from a choke hold in 2014. Chicago already enacted all policies from #8cantwait, including requiring "officers provide their name and star number", which was violated last week. Problem solved? Unlikely.

(@JohnArnoldFndtn)

Due to the desire for more restrictive methods, in combination with the George Floyd and past incidents, shortly after the start of the *#8CantWait* campaign, several cities took aim at adopting such policies themselves. Within a few weeks of the start of the campaign, the Los Angeles County Board of Supervisors was set to vote on adopting the recommendations at the end of June 2020. At the beginning of July 2020, the Atlanta city council adopted the *#8CantWait* recommendations, and in mid-September 2020, Charlotte, North Carolina did the same. At the beginning of August 2020, Berkeley, California approved to adopt the four *#8CantWait* recommendations as of October 1, 2020, noting that they were already employing the other four recommendations. Due to societal pressure, and media attention on the topic, cities quickly began proposing to adopt the campaign's recommendations, as a way to bring about change within policing.

The "Phase Out and Restart" Frame

A counter-idea offered by abolitionists is that the entire system of policing in the United States is fundamentally broken. This perception of reality has led many to define defunding the police as a key step in the elimination process, viewing policing as a system that needs to be torn down (dismantled) and started over (Vitale, 2017). A key issue with this approach, however, is a lack of ideal in how the criminal justice system would look if we dismantled it and started it over. Some argue that specific policies and laws would no longer exist (e.g., Three Strikes Law, mandatory minimum sentencing guidelines, militarized police), but they fail to fully demonstrate just what the system would look like, especially in terms of law enforcement roles. An extreme approach, as discussed here, is one where law enforcement and prisons no longer existed, and individuals policed themselves while providing needed public services for all:

It's time for a bold reimaging of the role that police play in our society. (@ACLU) ←— Led by the Movement for Black Lives, we are demanding an investment in: schools, communities, people. Not police. #DefundThePolice.

(@aclupa)

The "Phase Out and Restart" frame merges the concept of *#DefundThePolice* with those of *#AbolishThePolice* on Twitter. More specifically, the "Phase Out and Restart" framework being constructed here is highly similar to the "Opportunity Cost" frame which was uncovered within the *#AbolishThePolice* Tweets discussed earlier in this book. Most of the writers refer to Alex Vitale's conceptualization of abolishing the police, covered in depth within his book "The End of Policing" (2017), as well as citing Camden, New Jersey as a successful case of restarting a police force. As a brief recap, Vitale's central claims included the following:

- Decriminalizing activities such as prostitution, drug possession, gambling, and so on to reduce the scope of what police need to concern themselves with.
- Firing all current officers and hiring a retrained force which is "demilitarized" – one which is largely unarmed and expertly utilizes conflict reduction techniques.
- Creating a new police force which is numerically smaller than the previous force and with a reduced budget in an effort to reallocate funds to other community needs (such as providing social workers and mental health counselors).

This version of abolishing police recognizes the need for police but wholly rejects the current form of policing that is commonplace in the United States today. While highly critical of policing tactics and rejecting all notions of within-the-system reform, these writers also offer concrete suggestions for how to improve law enforcement and also see the need for a police force. These viewpoints stand in contrast to the "World Without Police" writers discussed in the following, who are hostile toward the police and reject the notion that there is a need to have a professional police force at all.

The "World Without Police" Frame

An even more radical approach to the *#DefundThePolice* are the abolitionists who advocate for a world without police and prisons. These individuals tend to believe that the criminal justice system is too far gone to be reformed, so getting rid of it completely would be better than continuing to have such a system. A core claim of this movement is that the more police there are, the more contact citizens will have with police, especially black citizens. This in turn will mainly deprive people of color from liberty, cause more arrests, increase imprisonment, and result in more harm and more deaths. It is argued that getting rid of police and prisons will better protect society, especially black citizens, from harm and death at the hands of the police.

A highly circulated claim, deemed "8 to Abolition", (a rebranding of the "8 can't wait" movement), calls for eight steps to be taken to create a world without prisons or police. These eights steps included the following (@Doctorow):

- Defund the police
- Demilitarize communities
- Remove police from schools
- Free people from prisons and jails
- Repeal laws criminalizing survival
- Invest in community self-governance
- Provide safe housing for everyone
- Invest in care, not cops

Those calling for a complete end to law enforcement, thus allowing communities to police themselves, state that getting rid of police does not mean they will abandon public safety but instead rely on the community to take care of one another: "#AbolishThePolice doesn't mean abandoning public safety: it's about replacing armed police officers with public services that perform the same safety roles" (@Doctorow).

A key example of a community getting rid of law enforcement and policing themselves can be seen in the Capitol Hill Autonomous Zone (C.H.A.Z.), which was created on June 8, 2020, in Seattle, Washington. C.H.A.Z. occupied six city blocks, including Cal Anderson Park, until it was disbanded on July 1, 2020. The area was barricaded off with individuals occupying it consisting of not only citizens of Seattle but also those who traveled to the area as well. A photo of what the C.H.A.Z. zone looked like, as well as a map which indicates how much of Seattle was turned into this zone, can be seen in Figures 3.4 and 3.5.

However, tweets soon documented that this attempt to self-patrol Seattle had gone horribly wrong. Within two days of being established, C.H.A.Z. had been accused by multiple Twitter users of having a warlord named Raz Simone running it:

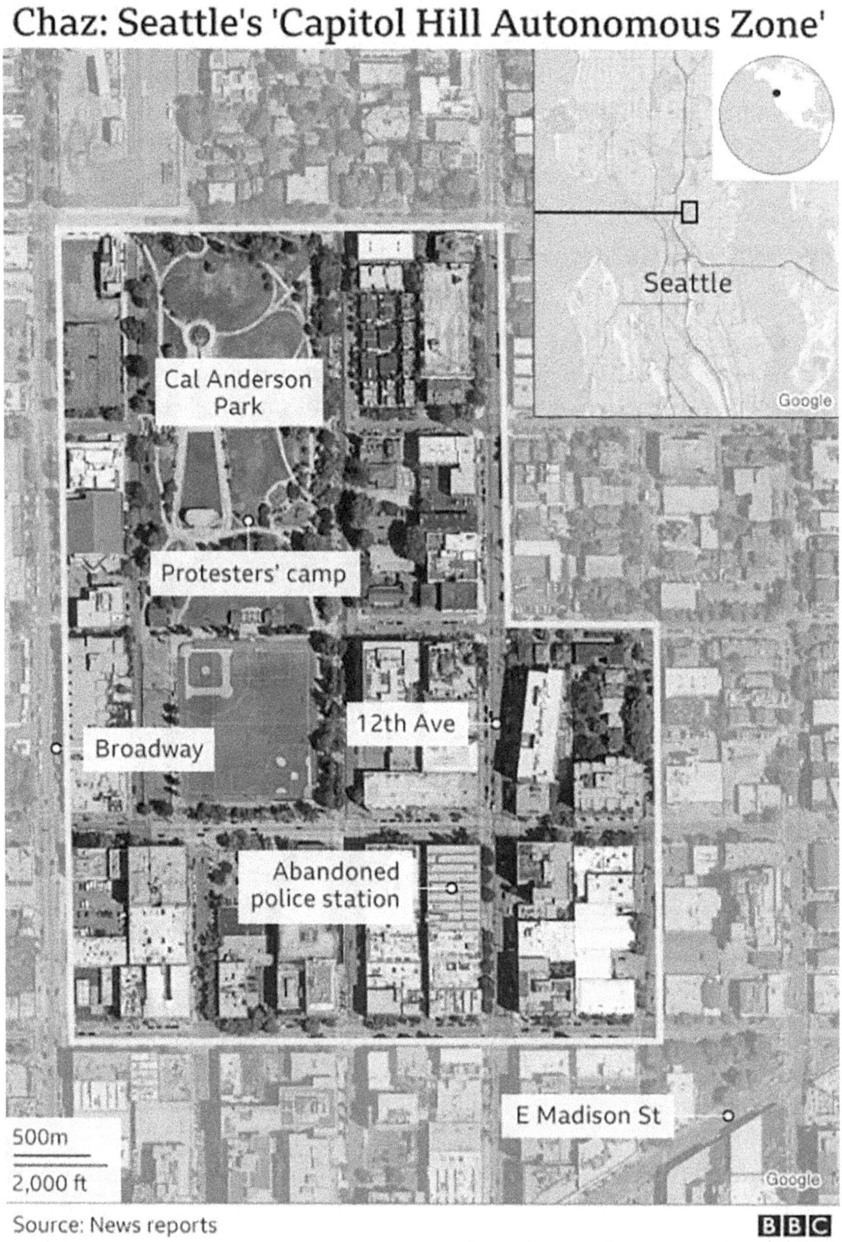

FIGURE 3.4

FIGURE 3.5

> When we #DefundThePolice we'll have a caring crimeless Utopia! . . . 36 hours later: Dictator-
> ship by armed Warlords.
>
> *(@KasimirUrbanski)*

Additionally, those who lived in the area were either kept from their homes or held hostage within
them, unable to move about freely. C.H.A.Z. was proclaimed an area free of governmental rules and
law enforcement, yet to come into the area, individuals had to show identification while protestors
occupying the area patrolled the barriers with guns in hand.

> Seattle #antifa extremists have occupied the Capitol Hill area in Seattle & turned it into a no-go
> zone. They have their people patrolling the barriers they set up. Local news crew was chased out.
> They had to see refuge in fire station.
>
> *(@MrAndyNgo)*

Such enforcement within the area drastically contradicted the intended purpose of the autonomous zone. Without law enforcement, certain groups took it upon themselves to act as the police
instead. As a result of a lack of law enforcement in the area, violence, rape, and other crimes rose,
making the area dangerous and unsafe for those within it. When medical assistance was needed,
law enforcement officers were prohibited from entering this area, even during medical emergencies. Local politicians allowed C.H.A.Z. to continue until the violence within it became too much.
Ironically, law enforcement officers were reached out to by the public, and then were tasked with
shutting it down.

Simultaneously, protesters in Minneapolis made a strong push to become a city without law
enforcement as well, in response to the death of George Floyd. By the end of June 2020, the Minneapolis City Council had voted to eliminate the city's police department and replace it with "a
department of community safety and violence prevention" (Romo, 2020, para. 7). This department
would consist of individuals with experience in community safety services, who did not have any

prior law enforcement experience. This plan, as will be discussed in a later chapter, failed. Upon voting to pass this idea, a high volume of law enforcement officers retired while others quit their jobs in droves. By September 2020, the city was experiencing a surge in crime, especially violent crime. As a result, by February 2021, the city was spending over $6 million to recruit more police officers.

These examples demonstrate that removing police officers and expecting a community to develop a safer and more effective police force in a primarily serendipitous manner is a misguided belief. Simply removing officers in a reactionary measure created unpoliced areas, which quickly became areas consumed by violent crimes.

Discussion and Summary

Those using the hashtag *#DefundThePolice* displayed a highly ambivalent approach to policing, and there seems to be at least three competing train of thoughts which coexist in this public sphere. One viewpoint endorses *#DefundThePolice* primarily as a punitive plan to purposely reduce the role and size of police departments as a rejection of police practices, which are viewed as both dehumanizing and ineffective at maintaining social order. Many of those using the hashtag in this way seemingly make no distinction between *#DefundThePolice* and *#AbolishThePolice* as concepts, thinking of them as interchangeable expressions. If there is any distinction between the two, defunding the police is mainly viewed as a starting point for the ultimate long-term goal of abolishing the police.

A second viewpoint depicts police departments as a social support system which has long been financially privileged in comparison to other public services that communities need. What follows is a proposed justification for reducing police budgets not as an act of hostility, but as a recognition of community resources being distributed inefficiently. This tone is notably more positive in opinion toward police forces and is made with a recognition of the need for policing. Nevertheless, the hashtag is advanced with an underlying assumption that their community role is too large and should be scaled back.

The third viewpoint within this hashtag sees defunding as a philosophical transformation about the nature of crime and punishment, viewing police forces as unnecessary. It could even be described as a public endorsement for the ideological principles of anarchism, where it is believed that order would ultimately be the outcome of chaos. These expressions seemingly are both ideological and politically opportunistic, taking advantage of widespread negative public sentiment in an attempt to overturn our cultural notions of why we need police. The abolish police movement generally identifies actionable steps as to how the end of policing could be achieved in the long run. In contrast, those within this mindset of defunding the police seemingly believe that all current forms of policing can end immediately in an informal, organic way – giving way to citizens as law enforcers without any formalized organizing or planning at all.

Additionally, even though a large-scale social movement is using "defund the police" as a talking point, very few individuals are actually providing any concrete, practical suggestions on how to go about carrying out effective police reform. Part of this reasoning could be due to the inaccurate definition society is giving the "defund the police" slogan. In sum, opinions within this hashtag ranged from suggestions for improvements, to accusations of police being terrorists, even examples of cities abolishing their police and establishing autonomous zones. Overall, there is tremendous variation of definition and perspectives found within this hashtag, which likely creates confusion and fear among the public, as it is highly unclear what *#DefundThePolice* means from one person to the next.

References

Arnold, A. (2020, June 12). What exactly does it mean to defund the police? *The Cut*. www.thecut. com/2020/06/what-does-defund-the-police-mean-the-phrase-explained.html

Bazaldua, E. (2016, August 2). Law enforcement officials say they are expected to do *'everything for everybody.' KLTV.* www.kltv.com/story/32603243/law-enforcement-officials-say-they-are-expected-to-do-everything-for-everybody/

BBC. (2020). *Protests also refer to it as the Capitol Hill occupied protest, or chop*. www.bbc.com/news/world-us-canada-53224445

Black Lives Matter. (2020). *#DefundThePolice*. http://blacklivesmatter.com/defundthepolice

Borum, R., Deane, M. W., Steadman, H. J., & Morrissey, J. P. (1998). Police perspectives on responding to mentally ill people in crisis: Perceptions of program effectiveness. *Behavioral Sciences & the Law*, *16*(4), 393–405.

Brashear, S. (2020). The Capitol Hill autonomous zone in Seattle. [Photograph]. *MRonline*. https://mronline. org/2020/06/18/revolutionary-ideals-of-the-paris-commune-live-on-in-black-lives-matter-autonomous-zone-in-seattle/#sidr-main

Caldeira, G. A., & Cowart, A. T. (1980). Budgets, institutions, and change: Criminal justice policy in America. *American Journal of Political Science*, *24*(3), 413–438.

Campaign Zero. (2020). *#8CantWait*. https://8cantwait.org/

Cobbina-Dungy, J., LaCourse, A., Chaudhuri, S., & DeJong, C. (2022). Defund the police: Perceptions among protestors in the 2020 march on Washington. *Criminology & Public Policy*, *21*(1), 1–28.

Cortright, C. E., McCann, W., Willits, D., Hemmens, C., & Stohr, M. (2020). An analysis of state statutes regarding the role of law enforcement. *Criminal Justice Policy Review*, *31*(1), 103–132.

Dionne, E. J., & Mann, T. E. (2003, June 1). Polling & public opinion: The good, the bad, and the ugly. *Brookings Institute*. www.brookings.edu/articles/polling-public-opinion-the-good-the-bad-and-the-ugly

Fyfe, J. J. (1979). Administrative interventions on police shooting discretion – An empirical examination. *Journal of Criminal Justice*, *7*(4), 309–323.

Hipple, N. K. (2017). Policing and homelessness: Using partnerships to address a cross system issue. *Policing: A Journal of Policy & Practice*, *11*(1), 14–28.

Jacobs, D., & Helm, R. E. (1997). Testing coercive explanations for order: The determinants of law enforcement strength over time. *Social Forces*, *75*(4), 1361–1392.

Lamb, H. R., Shaner, R., Elliot, D. M., DeCuir Jr., W. J., & Foltz, J. T. (1995). Outcome for psychiatric emergency patients seen by an outreach police-mental health team. *Psychiatric Services*, *46*(12), 1267–1271.

Murray, P. (2022, July 8). Partisanship drives latest shift in race relations attitudes. [Press Release] *Monmouth University*. www.monmouth.edu/polling-institute/reports/monmouthpoll_us_070820/

Normore, A. H., Ellis, B., & Bone, D. H. (2016). The defragmentation of mental health services, police, and the homeless. *Policing: A Journal of Police and Practice*, *10*(2), 134–142.

Onwauchi-Willig, A. (2021). The trauma of awakening to racism: Did the tragic killing of George Floyd result in cultural trauma for whites? *Houston Law Review*, *58*(4), 1–23.

Perano, U. (2020, June 7). Black Lives Matter co-founder explains "defund the police" slogan. *Axios*. www. axios.com/defund-police-black-lives-matter-7007efac-0b24-44e2-a45c-c7f180c17b2e.html

Reiss Jr., R. J. (1992). Police organization in the twentieth century. *Crime and Justice*, *15*, 51–97.

Romo, V. (2020, June 26). Minneapolis council moves to defund police, establish 'holistic' public safety force. *NPR*. www.npr.org/sections/live-updates-protests-for-racial-justice/2020/06/26/884149659/minneapolis-council-moves-to-defund-police-establish-holisti c-public-safety-force

Slate. (2020, June 19). *What three cities are spending on police compared with everything else*. https://slate.com/news-and-politics/2020/06/what-los-angeles-minneapolis-dallas-police-spend.html

Statista. (2017). Total police budget and share of cities' general fund expenditure in 2017. [Photograph]. *Forbes*. www. forbes.com/sites/niallmccarthy/2017/08/07/how-much-do-u-s-cities-spend-every-year-on-policing-infographic/?sh=5713a2fde7b7

Steadman, H. J., Deanne, M. W., Borum, R., & Morrissey, J. P. (2000). Comparing outcomes of major models of police response to mental health emergencies. *Psychiatric Services*, *51*(5), 645–649.

Tennenbaum, A. N. (1994). The influence of the *Garner* decision on police use of deadly force. *The Journal of Criminal Law & Criminology, 85*(1), 241–260.

Torres, J., Reling, T., & Hawdon, J. (2018). Role conflict and the psychological impacts of the post-Ferguson period on law enforcement motivation, cynicism, and apprehensiveness. *Journal of Police and Criminal Psychology, 33*(4), 358–374.

Vitale, A. P. (2017). *The end of policing*. Verso Books.

White, M. D. (2000). Assessing the impact of administrative policy on use of deadly force by on- and off-duty police. *Evaluation Review, 24*(3), 295–318.

4

PUBLIC DISCOURSE AND THE NATURE OF COMMUNITY POLICING

Introduction

The evolution of policing, as discussed here, has changed with societal standards. One of the most prominent and effective forms of policing is community policing. However, while effective, community policing is also tough to define. Cordner (1995) states that "community policing remains many things to many people . . . community policing is a philosophy, not a program" (p. 1). As such, it is no surprise that the definition society gives to community policing differs based on one's viewpoints of law enforcement and knowledge of policing. The following is a discussion of the evolution of policing including how we have come to define community policing over time and how society defines community policing via tweets containing the hashtag *#CommunityPolicing*.

History of Policing

The historical creation and shift in policing can be linked to as far back as ancient Greece and the Roman Empire. From the formation of the first public police force to the creation of the Peelian Principles, which laid the foundation of policing in the United States, we can see the issues and development within policing over the years. Such a history is important to understand the implementation of community policing, which is viewed as one of the most successful policing strategies in existence.

Early Policing: The Foundations

One of the earliest forms of policing, kin policing, arose in Greece and Rome. This aspect of policing, via enforcement of informal norms and behaviors, was left to the members of one's family or tribe (Roberg et al., 2012). Punishments for violating social norms were extremely brutal, reflecting the Code of Hammurabi – "an eye for an eye" mentality – where individuals would lose a hand for stealing bread (Roberg et al., 2012, p. 31). Over time, the responsibility of policing shifted from the responsibility of the family to appointed magistrates. By 27 BC, Rome had created *praefectus urbi*, or the first paid public police officer, which led to the first establishment of a large patrolling public police force.

DOI: 10.4324/9781003224440-4

The fall of the Roman Empire left the bulk of European society in chaos until the twelfth and thirteenth centuries, when kings took on the role of implementing law enforcement. Kings established the "Nightwatch", increased citizen patrols, and designated specific individuals (sheriffs) to make arrests and investigate crimes. A key example of this is depicted in the classic story of *Robin Hood*, with King Richard assigning the Sheriff of Nottingham to collect taxes and make arrests. Ultimately, this led to the Frankpledge System, whereby a sheriff grouped individuals within an area into shires (Roberg et al., 2012), making policing of a geographical area more manageable. In 1285, following a decline in the King of England's appointees successfully completing their duties, the Statute of Westminster was enacted, providing more authority to the constable, who was elected by the citizens of the parish in which he policed (Uchida, 2010). The constable, who was unpaid, was given the authority to investigate crimes and to make arrests, thereby making constables the first form of police officers.

Up until the 1800s, a county sheriff was responsible for policing their designated county, with assistance from the justice of the peace (established in England in the 1200s), who were themselves assisted by constables (Roberg et al., 2012). This was the style of policing the United States adopted during this time period. Due to the small, rural aspect of the US colonies, having a paid sheriff police the area was efficient. The specific duties of the sheriff, who was appointed by the governor for each colony, "included apprehending criminals, serving subpoena[s], appearing in court, and collecting taxes" (Uchida, 2010, pp. 19–20). A key issue with this form of policing, however, was the sheriff's pay was on a sliding scale, based on the tasks performed – so the more taxes the sheriff collected, the higher their pay. As a result, collecting taxes became the main objective of the sheriffs, with "law enforcement [as] a low priority" (Uchida, 2010, p. 20).

Nineteenth-Century England and the Peelian Approach

This policing approach was adapted in nineteenth-century England and is the basis of modern-day policing found in the United States. Henry Fielding, the magistrate for Middlesex and Westminster, was among the first individuals to believe that police action was more than a means to collect taxes, but that it could actually prevent crime – something past policing had failed to do. Due to such a belief, between 1754 and 1780, Fielding developed and implemented the Bow Street station (Roberg et al., 2012). The Bow Street station demonstrated features that are still commonly seen in modern policing:

> The station was organized into three groups that performed specific crime control functions. Men engaged in foot patrol in the inner areas of the city. Additionally, men on horseback allowed for patrol up to 15 miles away from the Bow Street station. Finally, a group of men were responsible for responding to crime scenes to engage in investigations. These plain-clothed men became known as the *Bow Street Runners* or "*Thief Takers*" and as such represented the first detective unit.
>
> *(Germann et al., 1978; Roberg et al., 2012, p. 32)*

In comparing the Bow Street station to more modern-day policing practices, we can see the aspect of specific crime control functions, where police departments, especially in the larger cities, have specified units to handle various types of crimes. We even begin to see, for the first time, different levels of policing (i.e., local, state, federal), where specific jurisdictions and duties are formally organized. In this early conceptualization of policing, foot patrol was considered to be the defining central feature of community policing, although in certain areas (especially for heavily attended events and populated areas) mounted units were used. Additionally, having detectives performing their duties as plain-clothed citizens was established and is still a common aspect we see in policing today.

In 1829, Sir Robert Peel, known as the father of community policing (Lewis, 2011), passed the Act for Improving Police in and Near the Metropolis (the Metropolitan Police Act). This act laid the foundation for current policing in the United States and led to the creation of the first structured city police force in England. Police officers (Bobbies) were disbursed throughout the city of London, allowing for officers to not only prevent crimes from occurring throughout the city but also be in proximity to locations when crime did occur. In creating a citywide police force, Peel listed nine principles, becoming known as the Peelian Principles of Law Enforcement, which continue to guide policing today. These principles are listed here (Williams, 2003, p. 100):

1. The basic mission for which the police exist is to prevent crime and disorder.
2. The ability of the police to perform their duties is dependent upon public approval of police actions.
3. Police must secure the willing cooperation of the public in voluntary observance of the law to be able to secure and maintain the respect of the public.
4. The degree of cooperation of the public that can be secured diminishes proportionally to the necessity of the use of physical force.
5. Police seek and preserve public favor not by catering to public opinion but by constantly demonstrating absolute impartial service to the law.
6. Police use physical force to the extent necessary to secure observance of the law or to restore order only when the exercise of persuasion, advice and warning is found to be insufficient.
7. Police, at all times, should maintain a relationship with the public that gives reality to the historic tradition that the police are the public and the public is the police; the police being only members of the public who are paid to give full-time attention to duties which are incumbent on every citizen in the interests of community welfare and existence.
8. Police should always direct their action strictly toward their functions and never appear to usurp the powers of the judiciary.
9. The test of police efficiency is the absence of crime and disorder, not the visible evidence of police action in dealing with it.

Modern Policing in the United States

Policing in the United States began in the early 1600s with the creation of the colonies, when English colonists brought England's system of policing with them. Over time, volunteer policing gave way to paid specialists and as society changed, the perceptions on what policing should be changed as well. As one example, in 1833, Philadelphia "created a [paid] 24-person day force and a [paid] 120 person 'nightwatch'" (Roberg et al., 2012, p. 34), producing a cohesive day-night police department – similar to what we have today. Five years later, Boston also created a daytime force to accommodate their nightwatch program, leading to other cities following suit (Roberg et al., 2012). Thus, the 24-hour police patrol and response became commonplace in the United States as a public endeavor established specifically to prevent and combat crime. During these early years, many of these police departments emphasized crime prevention over the apprehension of criminals. While doing so, police officers patrolled within communities as a way to prevent crime from occurring in the first place and to react and stop criminal incidents when they did occur.

However, more changes would emerge as the twentieth century arrived. According to Kelling and Moore (1988), throughout the twentieth century, American policing began to evolve across seven identifiable dimensions, as listed here (p. 2):

1. Authorization – The sources from which the police construct the legitimacy and continuing power to act on society.
2. Function – The definition of the police function or role in society.
3. Organizational Design – The organizational design of police departments.
4. Relationship to Environment – The relationships the police create with the external environment.
5. Demand – The nature of police efforts to market or manage the demand for their services.
6. Tactics and Technology – The principal activities, programs, and tactics on which police agencies rely to fulfill their mission or achieve operational success.
7. Outcomes – The concrete measures the police use to define operational success or failure.

Additionally, two key policing eras formed during the twentieth century – each incorporating and focusing on specific methodologies and policies. These eras include the political era and the reform era and are discussed in the following.

The Political and Reform Eras of Policing

From the mid-nineteenth century to the 1920s constituted a time era which became known as the political era of policing. During this period, the institution of policing was completely dominated by politicians, where policies were often primarily enacted based solely on the special interests of politicians. Powerful elected officials were fully in charge of approving all police hires, firings, and departmental policies, leaving police chiefs with very little autonomy of decision-making freedom. During this era, mass law enforcement corruption occurred at all levels, normalized, with officer discretion being influenced by personal biases favoring those in power.

In response to these severe shortcomings in American policing, the Reform Era of policing emerged in the 1920s and lasted into the 1960s. It has been argued that due to having developed the foundations of law enforcement professionalism, the Reform Era is perhaps "the most significant period in the development of policing in the United States" (Roberg et al., 2012, p. 40). The professionalism of policing helped to improve the behavior and performance of officers through the implementation of a code of ethics. Additionally, officer selection and training improved via stripping power away from political elites toward police administrations. In addition, the way in which departments were managed was significantly improved as well. During the reform era, crime fighting became the primary mission of law enforcement rather than acting as the muscle of political elites. Political agendas and personal interests of those in power were no longer involved in the decision-making process of officers or as the impetus behind new policies. Instead of politicians holding full control over the running of departments, where officers were not sanctioned for abusing their powers or engaging in improper behaviors, commissions consisting of citizens and experts were created to conduct investigations into officer misconduct and make recommendations for departmental change (Roberg et al., 2012).

A Breath of Fresh Air: Community Policing

The reform era ushered in a large-scale move to community policing, which is best defined by Willard M. Oliver (1998) as:

> A systematic approach to policing with the paradigm of instilling and fostering a sense of community, within a geographical neighborhood, to improve the quality of life. It achieves this through the decentralization of the police and the implementation of a synthesis of three key components: (1) . . . the redistribution of traditional police resources; (2) . . . the interaction of police and all community members to reduce crime and the fear of crime through indigenous proactive programs; and (3) . . . a concerted effort to tackle the causes of crime problems rather than to put band-aids on the symptoms.
>
> *(p. 51; Somerville, 2009, p. 264)*

This form of policing requires law enforcement to become more directly involved with citizens and interact more within the communities in which they serve. It was purported that, for law enforcement to most efficiently and effectively protect and serve, the input from the community members they serve is highly necessary. Community input allows law enforcement to obtain an understanding of what the community believes to be an issue to effectively address the community's needs. Additionally, with law enforcement and community members interacting with one another, positive relationships are formed, which increases community trust of police. Citizens support and identify with police officers as being the underpinning of a healthy community – where police officers serve the members of the community and abide by the norms within it. Such a collaborative relationship assists to decrease crime and increase community safety.

This iteration of community policing first arose in the 1950s as a way to improve public relations. These policing strategies included police–community relations, crime prevention, team policing, foot patrol, and Broken Windows policing. Police–community relations started with the creation of community relationship units within various police departments. These units started by presenting the community with public proclamations of the police's perspective on community issues and needs. However, over time, this one-sided approach to communication ultimately led to a more interactive approach, with the aim of providing community members with a platform to express their perspectives and concerns with policing as well. As a result, an emphasis was placed on police–community "communication and mutual understanding" (Roberg et al., 2012, p. 91).

One of the early focuses of police–community relations was crime prevention due to the community members enquiring on how to best protect themselves against victimization and to combat crime. Target hardening, or making a space or individual "defensible" against victimization through the use of alarms, locks, lighting, and avoiding risky areas and situations, became a focus of community education. Other crime prevention approaches also implemented during this time period included community crime prevention ("the assumption that if a community can be changed, so can the behavior of those who live there") (Roberg et al., 2012, p. 92) and situational crime prevention ("tailoring crime prevention responses to the specific characteristics of the crime problem being addressed") (Roberg et al., 2012, p. 92).

Team policing, which was first implemented in 1968 by the Syracuse Police Department, was also utilized in response to the riots of the 1960s. This form of policing is defined as "a group of officers, working as a unit, who are stationed in a neighborhood and are responsible for all police services there" (Roberg et al., 2012, p. 539). As a result of officers staying within one specific area, they were able to get to know the community members better while also allowing the community to get to know and become more trusting of the specific officers as well – a key aspect of community policing. This also led to the increased implementation of foot patrols during the 1980s, which increased interaction between officers and community members, allowing officers to be more engaged and a part of the community they are patrolling. With foot patrol, officers were able to employ what became known as broken-windows policing, whereby officers focused their energies on controlling and preventing minor offenses as a way to theoretically thwart more serious crimes from occurring in the area. However, this practice was not always well received. Community members began to feel targeted, even for extremely minor crimes, which negative impacted police–community relations and created a feeling of antipathy toward the police.

The 1980s also saw a broader approach to policing, where community policing completely changed from the more established definitions and practices. During this time period:

> [P]olice strategy and tactics are adapted to fit the needs and requirements of the different communities the department serves, where there is a diversification of the kinds of programs and services on the basis of community needs and demands for police services and where there is considerable involvement of the community with police in reaching their objectives.
>
> *(Reiss, 1985, p. 63; Roberg et al., 2012, p. 97)*

Essentially, instead of all departments following the same expectations and regulations, each department was now able to adapt their policing methodologies to whatever they believed worked best within their specific communities. For example, if a community was more concerned with drugs in the area, law enforcement would focus more on drug crime prevention as a means to assisting community members by fighting against drug usage. Likewise, if another community did not have a drug issue, police in that area would be able to focus on more pressing concerns within the community. By doing so, police and community members were believed to be able to work together in effectively addressing problems within a community, resulting in increased positive interactions and public support. Police officers were instructed to be more directly involved in the communities they serve, get to know the citizens better, which aided in developing public trust. Such actions were implemented to decrease crimes while simultaneously improving the quality of life within communities.

In gaining an understanding of everything community policing entails, it is important to examine the three main dimensions of community policing: (1) the philosophical dimension; (2) the strategic dimension; and (3) the tactical dimension. The philosophical dimension contains the main centralized ideas of community policing, including citizen input, broad functions, and personalized service. Citizen input involves community members having a say in policing, including what actions and policies departments enact, and to be a part of the discussion pertaining to when and how officers and departments are held accountable for misconduct. Broad functions refer to the wide array of responsibilities imposed upon police officers – including assisting victims, resolving conflict, providing social work, decreasing public fear, preventing accidents, and actively solving various community problems (Roberg et al., 2012) – in addition to the exclusive responsibility for enforcing laws and arresting those who violated them. Through adopting this multitude of additional community responsibilities beyond law enforcement and crime prevention, the relationship between police and the community became problematic.

The strategic dimension transforms philosophy into action by taking the ideas and connecting them to policies and programs. The "three strategic elements of community policing are reoriented operations, geographic focus, and prevention emphasis" (Roberg et al., 2012, p. 101). Reoriented operation calls for increased interaction of police with the community by decreasing patrols via vehicles and increasing face-to-face interactions with community members. Additionally, reorienting operations include performing necessary traditional tasks in the most efficient manner possible, so the time saved can be spent engaging in community-oriented events. Geographic focus calls for police to focus on where they are patrolling instead of patrolling based on time of day. In doing so, police should patrol all areas, including more rural areas, 24 hours a day instead of specified shifts, so as to always be present for the community. With the patrols, police should be permanently assigned to specific areas, so they can get to know citizens of that area, and vice versa, for trust between the police and the community to be built. Lastly, prevention emphasis emphasizes preventing crime by encouraging officers to not only engage in prevention methods (i.e., directed enforcement activities, citizen interaction, etc.) but also to identify any underlying problems within the community (Roberg et al., 2012).

Lastly, the tactical dimension "translates ideas, philosophies, and strategies into concrete programs, practices, and behaviors" (Roberg et al., 2012, p. 104). Positive interaction, partnerships, and problem-solving are the three most important community policing elements within the tactical dimension (Roberg et al., 2012). Having positive interactions with police can increase a community's trust in them and help to overcome the negative confrontations citizens have had with law enforcement. By forming relationships with members of the community which they serve, police are able to increase these positive interactions. In building positive interactions, community members are more willing to work with and partner with law enforcement. These partnerships provide the community with a greater say in policing actions and programs that are implemented within the community. The more police–community partnerships, the more trust between the two builds and the more crime and problems within the area decrease. By working with the community to identify problems, police are then able to use problem-solving techniques to address these issues head on, from both a policing perspective and a community perspective, which assists in building trust between the two entities as well.

As this discussion shows, community policing takes on multifaceted dimensions based on community needs, making it difficult to encompass the concept into a singular definition. Police departments throughout the United States employ some form of community policing, but no one approach is the same as another. As a result, the public tends to have difficulties in understanding just exactly what community policing entails.

In the previous sections, we set out to outline the emergence of community policing as both a philosophy and a tenable policing strategy. Given that this conceptualization of policing has existed for much longer than the other approaches examined in this book, we wondered if the public discourse on this topic would appropriately depict community policing. Our research questions involved how content creators on Twitter represent this concept, and if these tweets show an understanding of what community policing is according to criminology researchers.

Public Discourse Regarding Community Policing Perceptions on Twitter

Based on data collection of 200 tweets containing the hashtag *#CommunityPolicing* from June 1 to June 10, 2020, we set out to address the question of "how does the public define community policing?" Overwhelmingly, half of the tweets examined were tweeted by law enforcement officers or law enforcement agencies, demonstrating the core of community policing being enacted by law enforcement.

Overall, we identified five key frameworks that emerged upon analyzing the tweets which included the hashtag *#CommunityPolicing*. The remainder of this chapter will provide the readers with a detailed examination of how these frameworks were constructed, using direct quotes to illustrate central claims, as well as exploring assumptions that were made by the authors. We have given these frameworks the following titles and brief descriptions:

1. "Extinguish the Flames"

- Positive images are offered to counter the anger and hostility being directed by the public toward law enforcement from other sources.
- Police departments and officers respect and support the will of the people, even during the nationwide protests calling for police reform.
- The documented actions of police illustrate their support for the community and openly display how police officers care for the citizens.

2. "Citizen Policing"

- Community policing is conflated with the concept of abolishing the police, being used in a highly interchangeable fashion.
- Discourse over the pros and cons of a deprofessionalized citizen police force are exchanged by content creators.

3. "Troll and Co-opt"

- Community policing hashtag was used by liberal content creators to insult conservatives for their continued support of the police during the protests.
- Police reform discussion is often bypassed in favor of visceral political attacks of conservative Twitter users, using the hashtag to demean values and viewpoints.

4. "Demilitarizing the Police"

- Messages call for a return to earlier methods of policing, particularly involving police engaging in conflict resolution tactics that are primarily nonviolent.
- Messages often conflate community policing with defunding police, claiming that lower budgets will reduce the likelihood of police reliance on dangerous weapons.

5. "Start Over Like Camden"

- Community policing is used interchangeably with abolishing police, where community policing is incorrectly viewed as being synonymous with citizen policing.
- Citizen policing is largely viewed in a positive light and as an improvement to the policing practices currently in place.

The "Extinguish the Flames" Frame

In our sample, the most common frame used was the one in which police officers and law enforcement constructed content that was geared to reinforce positive functions of the police and remind the public of their emotional bonds and commitment to their communities. The *#CommunityPolicing* hashtag displayed content which displayed photos of police building goodwill, such as volunteering for community activities and charities. Much of this content was supplied by law enforcement officers and departments themselves in an effort to send a more positive image of police to curb the outrage taking place in protests around the country.

One such example was demonstrated by @HighCoSheriff. Photos of local officers attending a Boys & Girls club basketball event, playing basketball with the children were provided. Additionally, photos of one of the K-9 dogs socializing and being petted by the children were posted as well. Such photos, accompanied by the caption "The COPS ADAPT Unit stopped by the Boys & Girls Club in Avon Park today for some hoops. K-9 Benji stopped by, too, to cheer them on!" (@HighCoSheriff), help to display a bond between local law enforcement and youth in the community. A similar tweet used the #CommunityPolicing hashtag to connect with youth through sports, where police would play basketball, baseball, and other sports with community kids. The photo was an advertisement celebrating 15 years of P.A.C.E. – Police Athletics for Community Engagement. The tweet stated

> @PACEOmaha kicked off our 15th Summer Season of Free Athletics with our Annual Baseball Clinic – New format by age group to keep the numbers low as we social distance. What a great turn-out! These kids are ready to play ball! #OPD #community policing for 15 years! @OPDdcGonzalez.
>
> *(@PACE_Omaha_Tish)*

Likewise, tweets also included officers assisting a local lemonade stand, stating:

> While on patrol I noticed this lemonade stand. His mother is teaching him how to become an entrepreneur and that hard work pays off. We brought young Amir some lemons, sugar and suckers to help his business.
>
> *(@OfficerMorton)*

The general theme of these tweets is to reinforce bonds with youth, particularly minority youth, to counteract the wave of negative, conflict-oriented content widely circulating in other mediated spaces. In doing so, there was a clear objective of law enforcement officials to remind the public that law enforcement plays a supportive role in the community. This content was largely apolitical and devoid of any reference to George Floyd, police violence, or a need for police reform. While others used this hashtag as a chance to call for how policing could effectively be changed for the better, this content suggested that law enforcement is effectively serving community needs already. The content urged viewers to not villainize law enforcement but to remember that officers are supportive humanitarians who are committed to serving their communities.

While much of the content actively avoided any mention of the protests going on around the nation, some images were posted in which police were supportive of protesters, even supportive of their movement, while continuing to offer emotional support to citizens. These messages came from both law enforcement and citizens who wished to express their respect for police. The peaceful images countered other mediated content circulating with high frequency in mass media, and even on Twitter when indexed under the hashtag #AbolishPolice, which were continuously depicting the police as aggressive and violent with protesters.

Three usefully illustrative photos within this theme showed images of police officers peacefully interacting with protestors. In the first image, a police officer is hugging a protestor in Orlando while another protestor touches the officer on his shoulder, reinforcing a message to the public that police are not aggressive or confrontational. This photo, posted by the Orlando Police, accompanied the caption: "We received this photo from one of our citizens who witnessed an exchange between an officer and a young man during the demonstrations yesterday. Our officers are out here building relationships with the community. #communitypolicing" (@OrlandoPolice). It is important to note that while this photo was posted by law enforcement, a community member, further supporting the strong community link between law enforcement and the community they serve, sent it to them.

In a second photo, police officers are shown taking a knee while interacting with protestors in Bowling Green, K.Y. – showing they do not oppose their movement and are supportive of the crowd's right to free assembly demonstrating a peaceful protest. As @wkupd stated: "@BGKYPolice Lt. Col. Delaney leading from the top this morning as community members gathered in peaceful protest outside of BGPD headquarters. #communitypolicing @leadfromthetop".

A third photo was tweeted by a protester in New Orleans. This woman took a selfie in front of police officers on horseback, who were monitoring the area but were not engaged in any aggressive confrontation. The protester used the hashtag *#CommunityPolicing* to express gratitude for this peaceful approach and reminded viewers that police are not the enemy. The photo caption stated: "#NOPD and other police departments around the country, just protect and serve our communities. We are not the enemy. You cool with us. We cool with you! Let #bluelivesmatter be chill with @blacklivesmatter and peace will abide. #communitypolicing" (@TeeBurd).

Along with these photos, other content depicts law enforcement participating in the Black Lives Matter protests, such as the retweeting of a news article on a Flint, Michigan sheriff joining demonstrators in a protest and taking a knee along with protesters. In doing so, writers identify *#CommunityPolicing* as police identifying with the will of the public, supporting their actions, and always doing so in a peaceful and respectful manner. As expressed on Twitter are the following quotes:

Working together WITH our community is needed to bring out positive changes and solutions. Their voice matters in how we police. It's called #CommunityPolicing.

(@TheYogaCop)

#CommunityPolicing is #Peaceful communities that HELP #Police and vice versa.

(@PoliticsNewsUSA)

It takes brave officers to work in law enforcement. It takes *braver* officer to put down their weapons and walk side-by-side with the people of your community and listen. We can do better.

(@BriannaBytes)

Listening to the community enables law enforcement to get to know the members within the area, understanding what they perceive, value, and fear. It increases public trust and creates a positive relationship between the police and the community. Community policing is readily defined by the public in this hashtag as an approach which allows community members to freely tell officers about their issues or concerns, so officers can respond accordingly. This, in turn, results in law enforcement to focus its attention on whatever the communities themselves deem as troubling, increasing trust between the police and community in a positive cycle of trust and partnership.

Beyond the framing of police as supporting protesters through the distribution of peaceful images and content during protests, *#CommunityPolicing* was also used to demonstrate how social media can be used to collaborate with citizens to effectively fight crime. Content was not solely about resolving hostilities between the police and the public but also included concrete real-life examples of police and the community working together. This illustrates the utilitarian function of Twitter for law enforcement officers, acting as a reminder that social media technology can be used to forge productive channels of information with the public. Law enforcement officers and police departments used tweets to ask for the public's assistance to effectively police the community and solve crimes. Some examples found in our sample included the following:

> Today I've been tutoring SC ADDINGTON. First job – a report of a vulnerable OAP burglary that turned into a dementia welfare issue. Reports gone into social services to get the family extra help. Big thank you to neighbours 4 your help.
>
> *(@SWPCardiff)*

> Another stolen bike recovered by #roathNPT and lines of enquiry for suspects are being followed up, showing how the assistance provided by the community assisted police in recovering a stolen motorcycle. Other agencies encouraged individuals to report any suspicious so law enforcement can help to resolve the issue.
>
> *(@SWPCardiff)*

> NHT Found a Stolen Vehicle @SolihullPolice This Evening. Vehicle now Safe and Sound with Our Recovery Agent. If you see anything suspicious in your area, let us know and we will sort it for you.
>
> *(@StAlphegeWMP)*

> Our ward officers are working on what matters to the community they serve. If you have any concerns please let your team know, we can help resolve ongoing issues, short or long term problem solving. We are community to helping you.
>
> *(@MPSHaringey)*

> Been receiving reports of a homeless man in #Halstead. Thank you to the public who have reported concerns for him. He's been located & identified & with the help of the homeless team on @BraintreeCSP from @BraintreeDC we can try to get him the help he needs. #CommunityPolicing.
>
> *(@EPHalstead)*

The content within this framework constructs a positive depiction of law enforcement – one which identifies police forces as necessary, supportive, and emotionally invested in the communities they serve. It acted as a counterpoint to the maelstrom of negative images that were prominent during this time period in mass media content and even on Twitter indexed under hashtags such as *#AbolishPolice*. While the police were accused of being overly aggressive, institutionally troubled, and badly in need of reform, this framework of community policing reaffirmed a need for police departments while downplaying current public conflicts.

While five frameworks existed within the *#CommunityPolicing* sample, this was the one which most consistently endorsed the continuation of professional police forces. It stands in contrast to the other frames by fully avoiding the conflation of community policing with the concept of abolishing the police and contained the least amount of politicized discourse. Moreover, much of the other Twitter content indexing *#CommunityPolicing* holds a very limited understanding of community policing in academic circles and oftentimes writers made no attempt to define the concept, using the term mainly as a label for emotive expressions.

The "Citizen Policing" Frame

Many within this hashtag demonstrated a belief that community policing would be conducted solely by the citizens of the community, without the use of any law enforcement professionals. Among this grouping of tweets, approximately half endorsed a fully citizen police force as one which would make their community, and its citizens, safer. These views hold a high degree of overlap with the *#AbolishPolice* conceptualizations of police reform covered previously in this book, and often both hashtags were utilized in these postings. Some quotes which exemplified these perspectives are found among the following tweets:

> #DefundThePolice – Fund #CommunityPolicing and create safe and welcoming #PublicSpaces and belonging through community-driven #placemaking.
>
> *(@ebkent)*

> So calls to @DefundThePolice and #DISMANTLEPOLICE are not outlandish at all. We don't need to #police our communities – we need to ensure that people in our communities are safe!
>
> *(@KushlevPhD)*

> Imagining #communities without #police is not a pipe dream, it's a genuine plan. Communities must drive this agenda. We cannot rely on State structures to divest themselves of power. We must imagine a different future together & make it happen. #Abolition = a program for change.
>
> *(@crimsonchat)*

While posts were generally not filled with perceptions of law enforcement as an inherently racist institution designed to victimize minority communities, there was a sense that the police were beyond reform. Likewise, there existed a continuous stream of accusations that professional police were corrupt, violent, and not particularly adept at either preventing or solving crime. The mantra of "we can police ourselves" is heard time and again by those who operated with a firm belief that a professional police force was expensive and unnecessary.

Nevertheless, there were also a subgroup of writers who used the hashtag as an opportunity to play devil's advocate about citizen policing, questioning the feasibility and quality of nonprofessional citizen policing. Authors noted that the possibility of corruption, prejudice, and potential violence cannot be ruled out through the adoption of citizen policing and warned that a vision of community policing as a magical cure to these problems was unrealistic. One such tweet that demonstrated a fear about citizen-led community policing, especially within the LGBTQ+ and minority communities, can be viewed here:

> So my group of mostly #queer #white friends, with a significant #disabled presence, have been having a bunch of convos about the #AbolishThePolice movement. Biggest single thing that worried the most ppl about the idea of switching primarily to a #communitypolicing model was that we have all lived in #transphobic and #homophobic communities and the fear of bigoted neighbours mobilizing the community against vulnerable ppl, esp #queer, #trans, #disabled or #mentallyill ppl. Have ppl come up with solutions that would help mitigate those fears? The police deal ★very badly★ with all of those groups of vulnerable ppl now, absolutely, but the fear of what communities might do without the possibility of oversight is still frightening if you're in one of those groups, and this movement should be a positive improvement.
>
> *(@the_pale_queen)*

Likewise, the following post illustrates an example of how a community that is policed strictly by only citizens, without the presence of a professional police force, can actually fail and cause more crime.

> Years ago my town and surrounding towns disturbed by break-ins and ATV thefts held meeting for Neighborhood Watch. We never faced that before. Police were far away. The first 2 volunteers were later arrested for break-ins and ATV thefts!
>
> *(@phantom_final)*

Other stories pertaining to the negative impacts of a world without police included incidents where corrupt "Neighborhood Watch" volunteer groups were actually the ones committing crimes in their communities. Illustrative examples described incidents where the leaders of these groups used their title to act as cover to engage in criminal activity and even coordinated their actions with other members of the watch group, who acted as accomplices. Although citizens had banded together to protect themselves against break-ins and theft, those committing the actions were actually heading the protection group. This is a key example of how a world without police, and communities policed strictly by citizens, opens the door for an increase in criminal activity.

Perhaps, the most pointed rejection of citizen policing came from @abigaladams18, who provided a meme of George Zimmerman with the caption "This is who the left wants to patrol the neighborhoods" (@abigaladams18), reminding audiences of a high-profile example of how neighborhood watches can go horribly wrong. The meme consisted of a photo of George Zimmerman smiling with the writing "Replace police with neighborhood watches? Well, if you insist". Such a meme offers readers a stark reminder of the potential problems that communities could face by getting rid of their professional law enforcement officers.

The "Troll and Co-opt" Frame

On June 2, 2020, attempts were made by many on Twitter to block out supportive law enforcement postings and pro-Trump hashtags as a way to troll conservatives on Twitter as a form of social media protest. An attempt to drown out conservative voices on Twitter by hijacking the online dialogue spaces of conservatives was enacted by indexing reformist and politically charged leftist tweets with hashtags that are largely associated with pro-police conservatives. This strategy involved posting content tagged *#CommunityPolicing* in conjunction with a variety of other hashtags popular with Trump supporters, gun rights advocates, white supremacists, ardently pro-police groups, and anyone else believed to be defending the police on Twitter.

A motive for why police reform activists were doing this was explained in two photos tweeted by @aleasha_love, who stated "These are a few things to keep in mind if you want to use social media as a platform to protest. Found these images on Instagram from @/sa_lline #BlackLivesMatter #Blackout-Day". As per the shared images, the message on how to use social media to protest was clear:

> *Black people do not need reminders that Black lives matter. Let's target our posts towards the people that need to see and hear it. Time to use the algorithm to our advantage!*

> *Continue to post and share the truth behind what is happening. Optimize your posts by using hashtags that are geared towards your desired target audience (the oppressor). Think about where they would virtually hangout.*

What we found in these postings ranged from attempts to refute conservative claims to content, to insults of users with conservative values. While the content identifies exposing police reform calls toward audiences that are likely to oppose it as a way of changing public opinion, the content was largely inflammatory and politicized. Rather than using the #*CommunityPolicing* hashtag as a vehicle for educating the public about what community policing is about, it was co-opted by liberal partisans, being operationalized in a way that attacked political opponents in a visceral manner.

Also found within this group of tweets were authors who were conflating #*CommunityPolicing* with pro-conservative, anti-reform proponents, which once again transformed the concept of community policing into a political battleground. While grouping community policing with other pro-police tweets during the protests of June 2020, claims were made that community policing is no better than other forms of law enforcement. Community policing was equated with nostalgic calls for "simpler, old-fashioned days" of policing, which writers believed to be bad policing that was viewed as hostile to people of color.

Within this group of postings, no concrete discussion about community policing or meaningful discussions about the pros and cons of such a practice were held. Instead, the hashtag was used primarily for verbal conflict and to voice anger toward conservatives. While social media platforms enable the public with an ability to engage in reasoned discourse to remedy social problems, these messages largely squandered that opportunity. Instead, the hashtag was reconstructed into a digital space for political animosity, largely ignoring all academic literature on community policing to engage in verbal assault against conservative users. This dialogue seemingly acted as catharsis for those who were angry, trolling anyone they perceived to be unaffected by the death of George Floyd while continually voicing unswerving support for police.

The "Demilitarizing Police" Frame

This framework's primary focus was to connect police violence with the military-style equipment that police wear while on duty. Writers called for cuts to budget lines which provided police with various forms of equipment that were deemed as reinforcing a perception among officers that the communities they serve were extremely dangerous and threatening. The assumption made is that heavily armed police will inherently and naturally view a community with an antagonistic mindset, where acting with deadly violent force is reasonable and necessary. While the tone of these tweets is often highly critical of police actions, the overall theme was not angry or hostile but attempted to make a reasoned argument that there was a cause-and-effect relationship between police violence and how officers are equipped for their job. Some illustrative tweets found include the following:

> Defund the police? I haven't seen that case made yet. Demilitarize the police. Defund the line items that put military equipment in their hands for daily use. That's not for police work. That's for a police state.
>
> *(@revjoeyreed)*

Likewise, there was an open questioning about the wisdom of spending so much money on this type of equipment, where quotes such as "invest in communities, not armor" (@Dadtf2843) and "overspending to over arm" (@zungumuza) were commonplace. Moreover, the dollars spent on this equipment acted as a poor substitute for better police training. The following tweet is an insightful underpinning that many others echoed:

Police departments don't need tanks and other military hardware but they do need better training and better pay.

(@MythosaurusTex)

However, other than the shared concern about police mindsets, and that violence is avoidable through a demilitarization of officers on patrol, little else is said about police work. This is a generally simplistic use of the hashtag, as specific figures or criminological literature was entirely missing in all of the discourse. Claimsmakers largely envision community policing to essentially be the same institution, with the same officers and operational procedures, except without items such as body armor or automatic weapons being used in the field.

There is a presumption that police behavior will change in an organic fashion, as disarming officers will invariably alter the way that they relate to citizens. It seems that writers did not really have any real in-depth understanding of what community policing actually means to academics but seem to use the hashtag as a buzzword for apolitical, rational discourse about police reform.

The "Start Over Like Camden" Frame

A sizable number of tweets within our sample refer to Camden as a seminal case study for the success of community policing, viewing what happened there as empirically demonstrating that this conceptualization of full-scale police reform works very well. Writers within this framework called on their own local areas to now embrace this concept of police reform, viewing these actions as attainable and beneficial. Some specific tweets endorsing such changes included the following:

A case study too few know about. One city has already reformed its police department. It is possible. It can be done. Citizens and city leaders have to want to do it.

(@IveBeenMugged)

It works in Camden NJ and it can work in your municipality.

(@Mallenesq)

Community policing, & foot patrol has helped Camden, New Jersey; once the number one crime ridden city in America. During their protests of George Floyd's death, there wasn't any riots & looting.

(@kimedwards151)

As discussed earlier in the book in Chapter 2, Camden is often identified as a great success story for police reform advocates. In 2012, Camden was ranked as the most dangerous city in the United States. During the next year, the police department was disbanded by the city and replaced by a county police force, which followed a plan that is essentially predicated upon unarmed officers engaging in community policing practices. As a result of this change, a 62 percent decrease in murders was reached in Camden by 2019 (Vitale, 2017; Breslauer et al., 2020).

The recognition of Camden's positive results is typically assumed to be replicable by these writers, who believe that adopting similar approaches to their local area is certain to bring about improvements in crime control and overall police behavior. A prominent date within this sampling was June 7, 2020, which was the day the Minneapolis City Council, with a veto-proof majority, announced their intent to disband the Minneapolis Police Department. At this meeting, the council decided to invest in a nonviolent, holistic policing approach to emphasize public safety, without actually laying out the basics of this new method of policing. This news was interpreted by many as a signal that the council planned to follow Camden, New Jersey's previously implemented model. Tweets on this date largely consisted of positive opinions of this news, where people shared news articles covering the topic and discussing their excitement of what they anticipated to be better days ahead. The excitement about it could be found in the following examples on Twitter:

> Might this even signal the beginning of a trend? Possibly a seismic shift in the way "policing" is made to work in the future/to positively respond to the needs of changing societies/and to better relate to the local communities in which they're based. #communitypolicing.
>
> *(@ChaterhouseSq)*

> I can't wait to get the details of community focused policing. Are they disbanding the MPD and starting over with a totally different type of law & order policing structure?
>
> *(@attorneyangela)*

Time and again writers conflated the meaning of "community policing" with ideas that are generally associated with "abolishing police", incorrectly believing that the firing and relaunching of police departments are some of the founding principles of community policing. The viewpoints expressed by writers did not share the same emotive vitriol associated with race, violence, and corruption that were often expressed within the *#AbolishPolice* Twitter discourse but did agree that policing was in dire need of large-scale changes. In contrast, this discourse was a rhetorical repackaging of *#AbolishPolice* ideas, where a more civil tone and less inflammatory choice of words were employed to connect with readers. By doing so, the framework embraces an imagined audience defined by its rationality, with the motive to espouse police reform ideas in a serious manner. These tweets were optimistic and fully envision reforms as being easy to achieve successes, as writers encouraged readers to avoid complacency and pessimism and to embrace a creative approach to resolve the recurring problems felt about policing in the United States.

Discussion and Conclusions

In our sample, those who constructed an "extinguish the flames" framework exhibited a connection of community policing to Peelian principles. Also, they posted tweets in which police operated within the three core dimensions (philosophical, strategic, tactical), which were identified by the United States Department of Justice Community Oriented Police Services (COPS). Likewise, there were voices with the "citizen policing" framework which expressed a need for a professional police force, warning against notions that communities would be adequately patrolled by those who were not well-versed in this historically deep-rooted practice and philosophy.

However, a majority of writers seemed to have little or no understanding of what community policing really means, at least according to criminological literature. Many conflated community policing with abolishing or defunding the police, showing little or no distinction between these concepts and often using them in an interchangeable manner. The discourse of community policing was emotion-laden to a high degree among content creators, where there were common expressions of frustration and anger held toward the police. The hashtag was even used as a political battleground, where tags were made to troll those who supported community policing, based on the assumption that #CommunityPolicing was a space for pro-police conservatives.

While democratic principles favor the free expression of ideas in a public forum, such discussion lacks productivity when there is a general lack of understanding regarding the subject. In this context, it seems troubling that there is simultaneously a large public demand for police reform taking place in this online space, where those engaging in that conversation seem to lack a firm base of knowledge on the reform options they are either espousing or attempting to refute. Moreover, the content within this hashtag often reads as highly politicized, where it is fair to question whether those within this space genuinely want to find solutions or engage in conflict as a way to express their emotional outrage toward others.

References

Breslauer, B., Ramgopal, K., Abou-Sabe, K., & Gosk, S. (2020, June 22). Camden, NJ disbanded its police force. Here's what happened next". *NBC News.* www.nbcnews.com/news/us-news/new-jersey-city-disbanded-its-police-force-here-s-what-n1231677

Cordner, G. W. (1995). Community policing: Elements and effects. *Police Reform: Academy of Criminal Justice Sciences Police Section, 5*(3), 1–16.

Germann, A. C., Day, F. D., & Gallati, R. R. (1978). *Introduction to law enforcement and criminal justice.* Charles C. Thomas.

Kelling, G. L., & Moore, M. H. (1988). *The evolving strategy of policing.* Perspectives on Policing, U.S. Department of Justice, Office of Justice Programs, National Institute of Justice.

Lewis, M. A. (2011). Peel's legacy. *FBI Law Enforcement Bulletin, 80*(12), 8–11.

Oliver, W. (1998). *Community-oriented policing: A systemic approach to policing.* Prentice-Hall.

Reiss, A. J., Jr. (1985). Sharing and serving the community: The role of the police chief executive. In W. A. Geller (Ed.), *Police leadership in America: Crisis and opportunity* (pp. 61–69). Praeger.

Roberg, R., Novak, K., Cordner, G., & Smith, B. (2012). *Police & society* (5th ed.). Oxford University Press.

Somerville, P. (2009). Understanding community police. *Policing: An International Journal of Police Strategies & Management, 32*(2), 261–277.

Uchida, C. D. (2010). The development of the American police: A historical overview. In G. R. Duhman & G. P. Alpert (Eds.), *Critical issues in policing: Contemporary readings* (6th ed.). Waveland Press, Inc.

Vitale, A. P. (2017). *The end of policing.* Verso Books.

Williams, K. L. (2003). Peel's principles and their acceptance by American police: Ending 175 years of reinvention. *The Police Journal, 76*, 97–120.

5

SUMMARY AND CONCLUSIONS

This work has taken a deep dive into how people discuss police reform during the backdrop of high-profile incidents of police violence. The public outcry during this time period took on many forms: from street protests, to riots, to activism, as well as legislative efforts to improve law enforcement relations with the public. Those dissatisfied with policing have expressed their opinions thoroughly through their used of the "Abolish", "Defund", and "Community Policing" hashtags.

Our previous chapters have attempted to unpack some of the beliefs and perspectives related to policing in the United States. While an exhaustive analysis is beyond the scope of this study, several distinct findings may help to enhance future discussion on what social media contributions can tell us about how they feel about the police. Twitter content expressed many beliefs about the current status of police and community relations, the reasons to support/oppose various policing initiatives, as well as their perspective on the very nature of crime in society.

The following five thoughts to consider are not meant to be the final word on this topic, and future events will naturally unfold to further influence this subject area. These thoughts do, however, serve as a foundational launch point from which to cut through the often hazy and highly emotionalized discourse that is a constant thread on Twitter and similar social media platforms.

Five Thoughts to Consider

1. *The public struggles to understand what "abolish police", "defund police", "community policing" really mean and don't often make clear distinctions between these approaches.*

The three main policies explored in this book (abolish, defund, community policing) are often used interchangeably by Twitter users, indicating that the public does not largely understand these varied approaches as being uniquely separate from one another. From a policy formation perspective, lawmakers and politicians will need to better educate the public about how these policies are different from one another if they hope to successfully implement these reforms. For example, many Twitter users associate "defunding" as a short-term starting point for the ultimate goal of "abolishing" the police force in the long term. Likewise, community policing is often described as being

DOI: 10.4324/9781003224440-5

conducted by nonprofessional, unarmed community members who have replaced their paid police force – erasing any clear distinction between community policing and abolishing the police.

Making reform even more challenging is that these three conceptualizations of policing vary fairly widely in terms of public approval. While half of Americans favor "major changes" in policing, the most popular policies are less transformative in scope, where the public wants reforms in accountability and union protection rather than having fewer officers (McCarthy, 2022). In particular, abolishing the police is largely unpopular, politically speaking. Among 12 policy options offered to survey respondents by Gallup, abolishing police was the least popular option (McCarthy, 2022), holding public support that ranges between 10 percent and 15 percent. In comparison, roughly 35 percent of Americans are currently in favor of defunding the police (McCarthy, 2022).

Nevertheless, the tweets we examined indicate that these numbers may need to be taken with a grain of salt, since the public seems to conflate the two ideas together, as people often fail to see any distinctions between these approaches. At this point in time, "defund the police" – whose origins come from a call to reinvest money back into mental health care, counseling, rehabilitation etc., created to end law enforcement responsibility for responding to these issues – is often used synonymously with "abolish the police", which is less popular. As a result, policymakers looking to enact defunding strategies encounter opposition which associates these policies with abolishing police in the public mind – quelling the likelihood of successful implementation.

2. *Twitter is a space where outrage commonly takes precedence over reasoned discourse.*

Content posted under #Abolish more often functions as a shared public negative expression about policing in the United States rather than as a coherent discussion about police reform. Tweets overwhelmingly depicted the police as violent, corrupt, and ineffective. Users exhibited a large amount of anger, distrust, and perceptions of racist attitudes being held among the police. Some even claimed that American policing was rooted in slavery and is purposely designed to continually maintain structural and racial inequality in the United States.

While there are some who discuss how a community can abolish its police force, and why abolishing the police force is an improvement over their current condition, this was only a small percentage of the content indexed under this hashtag. Instead of Twitter being used as a space where this policy can be discussed in a reasoned manner by a well-informed public, it acts as a location for public frustration, anger and fear – looking more like a public critique or protest.

In general, Twitter is not amenable to discussing policy nuances or gaining a deeper understanding of complex social policies. While social media platforms have been championed for advancing participation in the new virtual public square, the price for such massive informational feedback can lead to an oversimplification of public issues, like crime or policing. This is understandable in light of the surface-level nature of social media platform. Twitter, until 2017, was limited to 140 characters, although it has now doubled in size to 280. Brevity such as this is certainly convenient but defies any kind of an in-depth dialogue on most subjects, not least of which is crime and policing. Instead, it is often used to broadcast viewpoints that lack ambiguity, sophistication, and complexity – replacing this with a mindset that there are just two sides to be considered, with one belief being right and the other wrong.

Criminological and related theories, such as those discussed earlier in this book, are crucially important to both the general public and policymakers to help make more reasoned and effective policy decisions for the welfare of society. Policy changes should be made in the area of improving our police practices. However, they ought to be based on sound theory and careful public deliberation, not as a quick reaction based on an ocean of negative emotions stemming from whichever high-profile incident currently taking place on television screens.

3. *Tweets consistently depicted police as being racist and having a propensity for violence.*

While it is not surprising that many viewpoints expressed about the police during the George Floyd protests were negative, there was a consistent theme of an "us-versus-them" mentality being expressed about the police – opinions which clearly existed well before the protests. It was disturbing to see how much doubt and fear were expressed about the police and how many people viewed them as more of a problem than a solution. Although the summer of 2020 was undoubtedly a low point in terms of public support for law enforcement, it is clear that there is a substantial amount of distrust and disconnect which exists at this current point in time – and has for a while. Even as public outrage has appeared to subside since the end of 2020, there is definitely work to be done by law enforcement agencies to rebuild community trust, as well as room to engage in self-examination regarding the use of violence.

Social media platforms like Twitter have become a space for widely expressing dislike, even hatred, toward law enforcement. Hashtags such as #DefundThePolice, #AbolishThePolice, #ACAB, and others have been used heavily by the public over the past two years to demonstrate a venomous distaste for law enforcement and to view their existence as a social problem in itself. Likewise, whenever a controversial incident occurs, many among the public tend to instantly blame law enforcement, or view them as being in the wrong, even when acting in a manner which complies with all existing laws and established policing protocols.

4. *There was a common expression that the status quo is not adequately meeting community needs, with a belief that exploring resource allocation for all social programs, including law enforcement, is a fair game.*

Beyond the direct anger being made by the public toward police due to the death of George Floyd, content creators showed overall dissatisfaction with the state of their communities, in general. Particularly within the "#Defund" and "#Abolish" samples, there was an outcry that communities were tragically underfunded in terms of education and counseling programs and had been for a long time. Within this mindset, policing became a vehicle to refocus public attention toward other community problems, using the moment to highlight these troubles by connecting them to police budgets, with the hopes of reallocating financial resources.

Again, while the public outrage about policing has decreased since 2020, the public debate about how to better distribute funds to meet community needs continues. How these contestations are resolved will obviously have an impact on the future of policing, particularly in regard to what resources are moved away from law enforcement. Future research may be able to focus deeper into the rhetorical devices found within the "Defund the Police" concept (on social media and elsewhere) which are aimed at redirecting the public's attention.

5. *All three paradigms had a group of contributors who wanted to abolish our current existing form of law enforcement.*

While each public discourse produced its own unique frameworks about policing in the United States, one theme which was consistently found in each sample was a call to abolish our current form of policing – with the main differences between these perspectives being what would take its place. Some contributors wanted a "redo", replacing current police with new officers – ones who were less violent and better trained. Others felt that policing should cease to be professionalized, replacing the responsibilities of law enforcement officers with the daily practices of ordinary citizens. There were even contributors who wanted to abolish police today with no mention at all of what would take its place – just an idealistic expectation that peace would simply prevail.

These content creators expressed a lot of cynicism about the likelihood of police reform, particularly voicing the notion that formalized institutions were incapable of responding quickly or effectively to public needs. A lot of frustration about bad police officers and practices being protected by police unions, department leadership, and various bureaucrats led to the fatalistic sentiment that police were beyond reform. The perception that these factors prevented reform often led to calls for a version of abolishing police which was no longer institutionalized, making it presumably more responsive and accountable. Nevertheless, this is not the concept of abolishing police that has been developed by criminology theorists or supported by researchers. It seemingly exists only as a form of wishful thinking – to imagine a world with no police, and no need for policing – which appears to be more of a utopian longing than an actual policy. This viewpoint exemplified a tendency to emphasize the negatives of policing and to scapegoat police officers for being a root cause of societal problems rather than as a response to them.

While the institutional apparatus pertaining to criminal justice was decried, there were feelings that other dysfunctional institutions also entrenched the problems associated with policing. Specifically, politicians and news media were viewed as further insulating the police from potential reform while also manipulating the public in their own self-interests. Political leaders were criticized for pursuing empty half-measures for reform, many of which had already been attempted (or even passed into law but not enforced) but failed to change policing. Politicians were described as largely in favor of the status quo, running from away from police reform ideas who half-heartedly pose as reformists only during times of crisis or public outrage.

Likewise, news media organizations are also viewed as posing to be reformers only during high-profile cases of police abuse. In the absence of visceral video content of police violence that outrages the public, news media rarely talks about police violence or call for reforms. Twitter content creators often depicted news media organizations as perpetuating a cycle of police violence, where a lack of sustained attention in the news to keep reforms on the public agenda ultimately resulted in more police violence taking place again, repeating the cycle of public outrage without policing reform.

Additionally, during this time period, there was certainly a high degree of overlap between news media content and what people were tweeting about, where Twitter seems to mimic both the content and the tone of television news. On social media, individuals shared official news media accounts at an enormous volume, spreading these narratives like wildfire, greatly expanding the outreach of typical news sources and increasing the consumption of this content.

It is clear that whatever mass media news was reporting, it is later discussed and retweeted at a large scale on Twitter – often retaining and amplifying the tone of moral outrage and concern about the lack of accountability toward police officers. What people see and hear in the news media about police abuse had a strong impact on the feelings and perceptions of audiences, but the production of news can lead to distortions as well. Likewise, distortions in fact can have serious consequences as well. When provided false or opinionated information, individuals then base their perceptions of the incident on such information, which in turn causes more public outrage and other actions, especially toward law enforcement.

News Production as a Barrier to Reform

The time period in which data for this book was collected took place during an extremely high point in public anger about policing, as well as a time period in which media coverage about police violence and reform-oriented protest coverage was continuous. At the time of writing this book, the news cycle is not currently discussing police reform at all, having been replaced by stories about other issues currently deemed to be more urgent and newsworthy. The lack of news coverage does not place police reform on the public agenda. As a result, public knowledge about policing, along with the reform options discussed in this book, will recede as a result of public discourse being greatly reduced. Reformers are in a conundrum about how to use this time – as attention toward police reform wanes after an initial period of shock and outrage due to other public concerns which emerge. While it is crucial to continue educating the public about what these policies truly stand for, the lack of public attention to the topic greatly reduces the ability to transform public opinion, which is likely necessary for reforms to be passed. It seems unlikely to believe that policing reforms will take place unless there is sustained news coverage on this topic, especially after the public outrage over a visceral case of police violence has subsided.

Another concern involves the accuracy of news media content and whether the framing of police as problematic is a fully accurate depiction of the situation at hand. Economic pressures can lead news media to have a "be first" mentality – as whichever organization can publish the information first will draw the most audience and will likely make the most money. There is reason to believe the pressures of producing news 24 hours a day, with an emphasis on constantly seeking new information, can lead to inaccuracies. News media sometimes makes mistakes in accurately portraying facts in high-profile incidents, which have the effect of reducing public trust and support for law enforcement.

One issue involves the broadcasting of cell phone footage of an incident without waiting for the body camera footage to be released. Cell phone footage often only records the aftermath of an incident, which runs the risk of audiences interpreting actions out of context. Providing the reactive recording instead of the body camera footage (demonstrating what happened from start to finish) runs the danger of providing the public a distortion of reality, where audience members are left without any knowledge of what led to the incident being viewed. As a result, public beliefs about police violence can be false, or at least filled with misinterpretation, based on incorrect assumptions being made by viewers due to a lack of knowledge about the situation. By jumping on the first bit of visceral footage obtained from a cell phone, without waiting for all information to be obtained before reporting an incident, there is a risk that the demands of providing quick news reports can lead to the consumption of inaccurate information.

News accuracy in the reporting of these high-profile cases were often blurry with key facts about these incidents. For example, in the Breonna Taylor case, the news media mainly reported that police entered the residence without announcing themselves, yet often failed to mention that the police were executing a no-knock warrant accurately within the construction of the law. Additionally, "various social media posts and media reports [had stated] Louisville police gunned down Taylor as she was asleep in bed" (Duvall, 2020, para. 23), however, as her boyfriend, Kenneth Walker in his statement to police, both he and Breonna had gotten out of bed and were heading to the front door before police had entered the apartment. As a result, she was shot in her hallway, as demonstrated by various crime scene photos. Even the number of times Breonna was shot was falsely provided, with news sources, including CNN (Andrew, 2020) and ABC News (Carrega, 2020) stating she was shot "at least eight times" (Andrew, 2020, para. 5; Carrega, 2020, para. 4), even after the official autopsy report had been completed two months before media reporting, stating she was shot five times (Weakley-Jones, 2020).

In addition, when it comes to incidents of police violence, media coverage emphasis often centers around race and violence, obscuring the underlying problem that police reform is necessary. Whenever there is a news story on a police shooting, the race of the officer and the victim are typically highlighted. Decisions about newsworthiness tend to be placed toward cases with white officers and black victims. By depicting police violence nearly exclusively within a racialized framework, there is reason for the public to believe that police violence is always racially motivated. Whether intentional or not, highlighting cases which involve only white officers and black victims has moved public attention away from policy options toward a view that police violence is simply a function of negative racial attitudes held among officers.

Along with a highlighting of race as a key feature of police violence, news coverage during the summer of 2020 also deemed acts of violence by protester. For example, the Black Lives Matter protests of 2020 tended to show primarily where riots had occurred, largely overlooking peaceful protests, as content involving violence obtains larger audiences. By doing so, violence and riots often became unfairly associated with the Black Lives Matter movement, which tended to negate the peaceful protesting (and the need for protests) that was the focus of the movement. Instead of seeing the Black Lives Matter movement as a peaceful protest for change, audiences were mainly provided with violence that occurred separate from the protests, thus providing a false narrative of the movement.

Lastly, it should be noted that bad policing is not always the central issue in policing controversies but that the laws themselves may be the heart of the problem. The role of law enforcement is simply to *enforce the laws* – laws that legislatures and the judicial system have created. In the majority of their actions and decision-making in everyday situations, law enforcement officers are simply adhering to the laws they did not create but then become perceived as the root cause of the problem when incidents occur.

As an example, in the instance of the Breonna Taylor case, law enforcement were carrying out a no-knock warrant – which legally allows officers to enter a residence without knocking and announcing themselves. These warrants are highly specific and are to be used only in situations where a typical warrant (knocking and announcing) is not feasible. No-knock warrants may be issued only when "an entry pursuant to the knock-and-announce rule . . . would lead to the destruction of the objects for which the police are searching or would compromise the safety of the police or another individual" (Legal Information Institute, 2022, para. 1), as per the *Wilson v. Arkansas* (1995) United States Supreme Court ruling. Additionally, it is up to the signing justice to verify the facts provided to them by the prosecutor, not police officers, before determining if such a warrant is necessary. In the case of Breonna Taylor, a no-knock warrant was issued, based on the criteria provided by lawyers and judges, where the preservation of key evidence was considered to be of extreme importance.

What seems to have been overlooked is that police were executing a tactic that was fully endorsed by the state. The United States Supreme Court provided the legal justification, the Kentucky state legislature signed the no-knock warrant into law, allowing for the use of such warrants in their state, the local prosecutor requested that a no-knock warrant be issued, and it was granted by the judge. However, it was only the police officers and the department which received the vast majority of backlash when a problem emerged. Had news media coverage distributed the blame equally toward each of these institutions, public reactions toward the police may have played out in a substantially different manner.

Politicization as a Problem to Policy Reform

While there are a number of ways in which news production may be preventing the public from developing a firm understanding of these theoretical approaches to fighting crime, our current political climate also acts as a barrier. More specifically, the politicization of law enforcement by liberal and conservative groups has become an obstacle to public understanding of what policing reform would look like and if it should be pursued. While discourse might potentially explore the positive and negative aspects of abolishing or defunding police, these terms have been characterized in polemic ways that are, at times, often detached from policing.

In some urban areas, abolishing the police was pursued in a fairly rushed manner by local politicians to appease the intense pressure to appease protests but also deflecting its community problems with crime and policing in a way which protected themselves from blame. One such example took place in Minneapolis, where the city council abruptly voted to abolish the city's police force in the days following the death of George Floyd. The local political leaders voted to get rid of their police department entirely in order to replace it with a more "holistic" approach to policing, according to council leadership. The issue, however, is that what the holistic approach actually meant, and what it may look like, had never been developed. Meanwhile, by voting to dismantle the police department, officers quickly departed – and with no replacements.

By September 2020, the city council had become concerned by the rapidly increasing violent crime rates in the city and openly questioned where law enforcement had been throughout the entire process, blaming the issue of crime on the police. In February 2021, less than a year from having voted to disband their police department, council members voted to spend over $6 million to recruit new law enforcement officers to handle extreme amounts of violence occurring in the city. As a consequence of a city council's hasty voting on a policing approach they seemingly had no knowledge about, Minneapolis encountered a skyrocketing violent crime rate, making it one of the most violent cities in the United States. It is an unfortunate situation that the city's police department will spend years fighting against, in an attempt to return the city to its pre-2020 violent crime rates. Figure 5.1 succinctly summarizes the comedy of errors in the city council's approach to abolishing its police force. At the time of writing, we know of no other city in the United States that abolished its police force since 2020 and duplicated the reduction of crime similar to what was experienced in Camden, New Jersey.

For some other liberal-minded political leaders, attention has been shifted away from police violence toward economic inequality, primarily focusing on the hardships of minorities endured in large urban areas. Rather than "abolishing" police in these communities, civic leaders instead attempted to reduce the role of police in their local area by simply redefining what would be considered crimes – tolerating public actions that had long been considered illegal. One example of this occurred in Seattle, where the city council introduced a "poverty defense", which aimed to reclassify all economic-based crimes (such as theft) as misdemeanors (Radil, 2020). The logic of the policy was to decriminalize actions viewed as produced by long-standing, unaddressed structural inequities endured by people in the community, who have "a right to survive" (Radil, 2020). Although this policy was ultimately not approved by the city council, the plan was seemingly based on the idea of reducing the quantity of interactions between law enforcement and the public, perhaps motivated by fears of police violence and racial unrest in their city.

Similarly, San Francisco saw a sharp rise in crimes during the pandemic, with viral videos of shoplifting taking place with complete impunity circulating online (Ortiz & Ward, 2021). Retailers in the area point to the passing of laws in the city which reclassified nonviolent thefts of less than $950 as misdemeanors, which they claim has "emboldened thieves" (Fuller, 2021). Laws such as these are reducing police encounters with the public while the city simultaneously maintains a fully staffed police department, acting as a half-measure of reduced police roles without budget cuts. Likewise, political leaders in the area deny that shoplifting is occurring at high levels, attempting to persuade the public that crime is under control (Ortiz & Ward, 2021). In each of these cities, there appears to be a political motivation to reduce the visibility of police in their communities, perhaps due to the

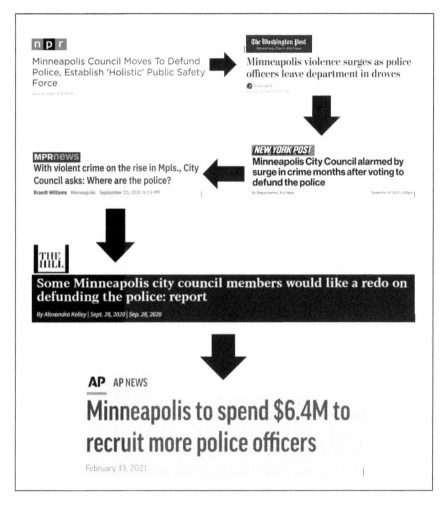

FIGURE 5.1

perception that the voting public wishes to see less policing in their area. Actions have been taken by Democrat policymakers to reduce the role of law enforcement, but none have apparently resulted in reduced crime rates, nor significantly improved the quality of life for their constituents.

On the other side of the political aisle, conservative politicians have used the terms "abolish" and "defund" as code words for radicalism, depicting even the discussion of police reform as subversive, absurd, anti-order, anti-police extremism. Since 2020, conservative politicians have used the relatively low support for abolishing or defunding police, according to polling numbers, rhetorically as a way of avoiding any police reforms at all while also associating reformists as being dangerous and problematic. For example, Figure 5.2 is a highly circulated image of Ted Cruz (R-Texas) at the Supreme Court confirmation hearing of Ketanji Brown Jackson during March 2022, waving the book *The End of Policing* at her on the senate floor. The imagery was produced with the intent of associating her with support for abolishing the police in the minds of the viewers, which is untrue.

Unfortunately, this was not the last time that the vague definition of these terms would be manipulated for political reasons. Images and language which dishonestly misrepresented the stances of Democratic politicians regarding "defund the police" to disillusion the public were "rampant"

FIGURE 5.2

during the 2022 election year in the United States (Dale, 2022). These ads run the gamut of offenses – from mischaracterizing votes, misquoting opponents, and even ads that "simply make things up" (Dale, 2022). The volume of these ads as well as the number of Democrat politicians targeted make it clear that this collection of messages was a conscientious attempt by the Republican party to misinform the public about what defunding the police means for election gains, using fear and outrage as motivations for potential voters.

Regardless of where one's identity stands on the political spectrum, the political climate acts as a barrier for public understanding about these criminological theories. Politicians all-too-often attempt to co-opt terms like "abolish" or "defund" to either champion other equity-based values or villainize any discussion of these ideas, often using fear as a motivation to reject change. Either way, the public is likely to remain highly uninformed about the positives and negatives of these policy approaches while discussing them with one another in a volatile manner which mimics the discourse they observe in mass media messages produced by political elites.

Final Thought

While our research was primarily a one-time snapshot about how people felt about police reform during a time period of widespread public outrage, these frameworks will impact how the public will be likely to interpret future events on this topic. At the moment, public demands for sweeping, immediate reforms have currently disappeared from the national news cycle, while also seeming to draw little attention from our political leaders. Nevertheless, the likelihood that a new instance of police violence will be captured on video in the future, sparking another emotionally charged national response from audiences, remains high. By understanding which frameworks already exist within this discursive arena, citizens and policymakers alike will be better able to interpret what the public believes and which policies they may wish to support.

What people believe and how they feel are influenced by their experiences and are not fixed entities but rather exist as fluid and ever-changing. As new events are witnessed and discussed about a topic over time, people alter their beliefs and, likely, their actions as well. However, frameworks can provide us with an ability to better understand how people will be likely to interpret this new information and can be predictive for how people will think and feel about those future instances – and suggest there is some stability regarding their attitude on the topic.

Of course, we certainly hope there will be no more disturbing videos of police officers fatally attacking unarmed black Americans in the future. But if this optimistic wish proves untrue, we aim for readers to be empowered during future news cycles by holding knowledge of these frames, being able to sort out information well and to question more effectively what they see and hear from others.

References

Andrew, S. (2020, May 21). The FBI has opened an investigation into the shooting death of Kentucky EMT Breonna Taylor. *CNN News*. www.cnn.com/2020/05/21/us/ breonna-taylor-death-police-changes-trnd/index.html

Carrega, C. (2020, May 22). FBI opens an investigation into the death of Breonna Taylor. *ABC News*. https://abcnews.go.com/US/fbi-opens-investigation-death-breonna-taylor/story?id=70829091

Dale, D. (2022, October 23). Fact check: The GOP's dishonesty-filled barrage of 'defund the police' attack ads. *CNN News*. www.cnn.com/2022/10/23/politics/fact-check-defund-the-police-ads-2022-midterms

Duvall, T. (2020, June 16). Fact check 2.0: Separating the truth from the lies in the Breonna Taylor police shooting. *Louisville Courier Journal*. www.courier-journal.com/story/news/crime/2020/06/16/breonna-taylor-fact-check-7-rumors-wrong/5326938002/

Fuller, T. (2021, May 21). San Francisco's shoplifting surge. *The New York Times*. www.nytimes.com/2021/05/21/us/san-francisco-shoplifting-epidemic.html

Gaynor, J. (2022, March 23). *Thanks to Ted Cruz, the end of policing is a bestseller*. https://lithub.com/thanks-to-ted-cruz-the-end-of-policing-is-a-bestseller/

Lartey, J. (2020, August 8). Why it's not so simple to arrest the cops who shot Breonna Taylor. *The Marshall Project*. www.themarshallproject.org/2020/08/08/why-it-s-not-so-simple-to-arrest-the-cops-who-shot-breonna-taylor

Legal Information Institute. (2022). *No-knock warrant*. www.law.cornell.edu/wex/no-knock_warrant

McCarthy, J. (2022, May 27). Americans remain steadfast on police reform needs in 2020. *Gallup*. https://news.gallup.com/poll/393119/americans-remain-steadfast-policing-reform-needs-2022.aspx

Ortiz, E., & Ward, J. (2021, July 14). After San Francisco shoplifting video goes viral, officials argue thefts aren't rampant. *NBC News*. www.nbcnews.com/news/us-news/after-san-francisco-shoplifting-video-goes-viral-officials-argue-thefts-n1273848

Radil, A. (2020, December 8). Seattle looks at new 'poverty defense' for misdemeanors. *NPR*. www.kuow.org/stories/seattle-looks-at-new-poverty-defense-for-misdemeanors

Weakley-Jones, B. (2020). *Coroner's investigative report: Breonna Taylor*. https://louisville-police.org/DocumentCenter/View/1816/PIU-20–019-Medical-Reports

INDEX

For Product Safety Concerns and Information please contact our EU
representative GPSR@taylorandfrancis.com
Taylor & Francis Verlag GmbH, Kaufingerstraße 24, 80331 München, Germany

www.ingramcontent.com/pod-product-compliance
Ingram Content Group UK Ltd.
Pitfield, Milton Keynes, MK11 3LW, UK
UKHW030829080625
459435UK00014B/586